# Christianity
# and Politics

# Christianity and Politics

## Catholic and Protestant Perspectives

Richard John Neuhaus          Michael Novak
James V. Schall, S.J.          Whittle Johnston
David Little                   Timothy L. Smith

Edited by Carol Friedley Griffith

Ethics and Public Policy Center
Washington, D.C.

**Library of Congress Cataloging in Publication Data**
Main entry under title:
Christianity and politics.
   Includes bibliographical references and index.
   1. Sociology, Christian—Addresses, essays, lectures.
2. Ethics — Addresses, essays, lectures.   3. Social
ethics — Addresses, essays, lectures.   I. Neuhaus,
Richard John.   II. Griffith, Carol Friedley, date.
BT738.C477          261.7                 81-19492
ISBN 0-89633-050-8                        AACR2

**$5.00**

# Contents

# Foreword

TWO WEEKS BEFORE ELECTION DAY 1980, on October 20, fifteen mainline Protestant leaders issued an unusual statement on Christianity and politics. It said in part: "There is no place in a Christian manner of life for arrogance, manipulation, subterfuge, or holding others in contempt." Few would take exception to these words, but some might say they were too narrowly applied. They were directed not to all Christians but solely to the new religious right. The Methodist, Lutheran, Baptist, Presbyterian, and United Church of Christ executives who signed the statement were clearly upset with Moral Majority and other conservative religious leaders for attempting to influence the presidential and congressional elections.

Gary Jarmin of the Christian Voice lobby, one of the groups under attack, shot back with some sharp words for what he called "extraordinarily hypocritical" establishment church leaders who "creep around the corridors of Congress with their collars on backwards, claiming to represent the Lutheran Church or the United Church of Christ or whatever." He said he would wager that 99 per cent of the members of their denominations "don't have the faintest idea" what these leaders stand for.

This is not the place to examine the interesting question of whether liberal or conservative church leaders' pronouncements on public issues better represent the views of the church members who pay their salaries. We can, however, note the irony of the spectacle. If one group of religious leaders has a right to press for U.S. withdrawal from the Panama Canal, unilateral nuclear arms restraint, and abortion on demand, surely another group has an equal right to take opposing views. Such differences and the debate they generate are as American as the New England meeting house and circuit-riding preachers.

Neither the old religious left nor the new religious right is blameless in its application of Christian morality to contemporary problems. Established agencies like the World Council of Churches and the National Council of Churches and their principal constituent bodies have been influenced to an alarming degree by a version of "liberation theology" that in its diagnosis of the world's ills bears a striking resemblance to Marxist thought. In many cases their pronouncements and actions on the controversial issues of justice, freedom, and poverty have diluted if not ignored the rich heritage of Christian ethics rooted in the writings of St. Augustine, St. Thomas Aquinas, Martin Luther, John Calvin, and more recent thinkers.

Evangelical and fundamentalist Christians, particularly those whose interest in public issues is recent, often claim to derive their views directly from the Bible. They too dilute or ignore the classical Christian social teachings. What we need, as Professor Paul Ramsey has repeatedly emphasized, is a renewed Christian ethic that is faithful to the great theologians of the past and relevant to the perplexing problems of the present.

It was in the pursuit of such an ethic that this symposium on Christianity and politics was conceived. The first two essays deal broadly with the relation of a Christian ethic to the political and social order, one from a Protestant and the other from a Roman Catholic perspective. The four chapters that follow apply the Christian ethic to particular areas of public policy.

Richard Neuhaus, a Lutheran pastor, theologian, and social philosopher, examines the impact of religion on American culture and concludes that the mainline Protestant churches have by default lost their leadership position in American society. Among the possible candidates for the role, he finds evangelical Protestants in the best position to provide "moral legitimation and definition to the American experiment."

Father James Schall, S.J., professor of government at Georgetown University, examines the development of Catholic social theory, with particular attention to the views of Popes Leo XIII and John Paul II. Conservatism, he says, is both intellectually and politically stronger today than at any previous time in the modern era, in part because contemporary secular liberalism and socialism are spiritually vacuous and have been proved unsuccessful in practice. Catholic intellectuals in Latin American countries are "the only ones who do not seem to know that Marxism is dead," says Schall.

David Little, who teaches religion at the University of Virginia, contrasts the positions of Jerry Falwell and the new religious right on legislating morality with those of an earlier Christian dissenter, Roger Williams, a Puritan forerunner of evangelical Protestantism. He considers the stance of the new religious right "a serious threat to the fundamental principles of a religiously pluralistic civil society like ours, and to the proper role of Christians in such a society."

Michael Novak, a Catholic lay theologian, a political philosopher, and a resident scholar at the American Enterprise Institute, addresses the relation between Christianity and democratic capitalism. He concludes that democracy and the competitive market take into account the Christian doctrines of sin and grace more than do any alternative political or economic systems. In the pre-industrial era, says Novak, the moral concern was rightly with just distribution, but today we must develop a "theology of economics" that also emphasizes production, fueled by need and fostered by invention and creativity.

Whittle Johnston, professor of government and foreign affairs at the University of Virginia, comes to grips with the perennial problem of power in foreign policy and world politics. Drawing on the classical Christian concepts of the just war and the responsible use of power, he focuses on the contemporary struggle between totalitarianism, represented by the Soviet Union, and the democratic West and its allies. He, too, notes the moral bankruptcy of Marxism-Leninism, and he insists that the United States by virtue of its power, wealth, and cultural heritage must take strong measures to defend the shrinking perimeters of freedom in a dangerous world.

Timothy Smith, who teaches history at the Johns Hopkins University, finds that much of the argument about religion in American education is based on myths. He concludes, contrary to these myths, that (1) church-sponsored schools have not neglected the social and vocational needs of their students, (2) public schools in the mid-nineteenth century were not wholly secularized, (3) church schools set up in immigrant communities did not retard Americanization, and (4) public funds have repeatedly been used to support private schools in the nineteenth and twentieth centuries.

These ideas and many more were advanced at a conference called "Christianity and Politics: Competing Views," sponsored by the Ethics and Public Policy Center in May 1981, where the authors and some 140 other persons engaged in a day and a half of lively debate. This volume consists of edited versions of the six key presentations at this first in what is expected to be an annual series of conferences on religion and politics.

Both the conference and this symposium are intended to stimulate constructive and critical thinking within the American religious community and beyond on our common goals of achieving greater justice, freedom, and order in a society challenged by totalitarianism from without and assailed by moral confusion from within. The Center operates on the premise that the great majority of Americans share a cluster of core goals bequeathed to us by the Judeo-Christian tradition, the Magna Carta, and the founding fathers of our republic.

On behalf of the Ethics and Public Policy Center I want to thank the conference speakers, who kindly gave us permission to publish edited versions of their lectures, and Carol Friedley Griffith, the Center's editor, who put the volume together with her usual consummate skill.

As in all Center publications, the ideas and views expressed are those of the authors alone.

ERNEST W. LEFEVER, President
Ethics and Public Policy Center

Washington, D.C.
December 1, 1981

# The Post-Secular Task
# Of the Churches

RICHARD JOHN NEUHAUS

I BEGIN WITH A BIAS. I will not argue it but simply state it: religion is the heart of culture, culture is the form of religion, and politics is a function of culture. That way of putting things is reminiscent of Paul Tillich, but the assumptions behind the bias could as well be attributed to Durkheim or Hegel or even to the philosophers of antiquity. Religion, the binding beliefs of a people, is, generally speaking, the dominant factor in how they order their life together.

Since the launching of the American experiment in the seventeenth century the formative belief system has been Puritan Protestantism. The lineal descendants of the Puritan tradition are today described as the mainline, liberal, or ecumenical Protestant denominations. If they and their world-views can be symbolically located anywhere, it is at 475 Riverside Drive, New York City, the headquarters of the National Council of Churches. The Council, though it has an admixture of some Orthodox and Lutheran Christians, is essentially mainline Protestant. It is dominantly supported and controlled by three groups—the Methodists, the Presbyte-

*Richard John Neuhaus is a senior fellow of the Council on Religion and International Affairs and the editor of a monthly commentary on religion and culture. Formerly the pastor of Church of St. John the Evangelist in Brooklyn, he now is a "pastor on assignment" for the Association of Evangelical Lutheran Churches. Among his books is "Christian Faith and Public Policy."*

1

rians, and the United Church of Christ. An alternative way of locating the Puritan mainline is in the Consultation on Church Union, which emerged from the 1960 "Blake-Pike proposal." It involves ten churches, including three black Methodist churches, in the search for an institutional unity to reflect the theological unity they believe they already possess.

Not all mainline Protestants are in any precise theological or historical sense Puritan. The Episcopalians, for example, are aligned historically with the Church of England, the very body against which Puritanism defined itself. By saying these mainline churches are in the Puritan tradition I mean that in America they have accepted the culture-forming tasks that can be traced back to the country's Puritan beginnings. Historically, they represent thoroughly Americanized Christianity and the effort to Christianize America.

Another way to define the mainline is to say who is not in it. The 50 million Americans who say they are Roman Catholic are not in the mainline. The 20 million who call themselves Lutheran are not, for the most part, in the mainline. The 30 or more million who describe themselves as evangelical or fundamentalist are not in the mainline. In short, most Christians in America are not mainline Protestants. Numerically, the mainline is not the mainline.

The majority of Christians do not belong to churches that have participated in the Puritan enterprise of defining America. In sociological jargon, these churches have not been agents of moral legitimation for the American experiment. My contention is that mainline Protestantism has largely abdicated that legitimizing task. Social legitimation is a task performed by elites. The Italian social theorist Wilfredo Pareto wrote about "the circulation of elites." When an elite no longer fulfills its function, the function—whether economic, political, or ideological—still needs to be done. It therefore circulates to another, usually quite different, group. And thus a new elite comes into existence.

This is one of the major shifts we are currently experiencing in American religion and life. The groups outside the mainline—Roman Catholic, Lutheran, evangelical, and fundamentalist—have been outside or marginal to the function of giving moral legitimation and definition to the American experiment. They have not been at bat. It may be their turn, since, as I shall argue, the mainliners who have been at bat appear to have struck out. For all of their crudities, maybe because of them, Moral Majority and the religious new right have kicked a trip wire and set off the alarm alerting us to these major changes.

The circulation of elites is not a smooth or mechanical process. There are ambiguities and uncertainties. The mere fact that Catholicism has not been at bat does not mean it is ready to assume the culture-forming tasks in America. It may lack the self-confidence required for aggressive culture-formation. Or its leadership may have imitated and become captive to mainline Protestant thinking to such an extent that Catholicism has disqualified itself before it ever got its turn. Both theologically and in terms of the immigrant experience, Lutheranism is close to Catholicism. Unlike Catholics, however, some Lutherans do think of themselves as mainline Protestants. Also unlike Catholics, the Lutherans find their tradition offers few conceptual resources for the tasks of culture-formation.

So also the evangelical situation is mixed. The communications media, even much of the religious media, frequently treat evangelicals and fundamentalists as though they were the same thing. In truth the evangelical world is diverse. Its central institutional grouping is the Southern Baptist Convention, and the centrist voice of its theological and social views is thought to be *Christianity Today*. (It might be argued that centrist thought among Baptists is better represented by their several state publications and lacks any national voice—which would be appropriate to the Baptist passion for decentralization.) I do not think it is helpful to follow Gallup and others in counting as an evangelical anyone who subscribes to a few selected religious propositions. That way one ends up, like Gallup, in deciding that a sizable proportion of Roman Catholics, Lutherans, Presbyterians, and others are in fact evangelicals.

Evangelicalism in its diversity includes the overwhelming majority of black Christians in this country. It includes some on the political left, as represented by *Sojourners* magazine. And it generally includes those of a strong Calvinist bent, as articulated in the

*Reformed Journal*. In my view, the most impressive network of first-principle thinking about Christianity and society is to be found today among those who identify with the Calvinist tradition. I think especially of the work being done at places like Gordon, Wheaton, and Calvin colleges, plus Fuller Seminary.

Fundamentalism has been a dirty word in culturally respectable circles for a long time. For that reason, at least in part, some fundamentalists preferred to be called evangelicals. But now fundamentalism is becoming distinguishable from—and is inclined to distinguish itself from—the larger category of evangelical. The fundamentalism that is the religious base of the religious new right is marked by a militantly rigorous commitment to biblical inerrancy and a reading of history that is shaped by a very literal dispensationalist apocalyptic. Theologically and sociologically, this fundamentalism is the polar opposite of mainline Protestantism. It is not unusual in the circulation of elites that the function's movement is not only to a different group but to an antithetical group.

These then are the four groups that have not been at bat but may be coming to bat. (I have not mentioned the classic Pentecostalists —as distinct from charismatic movements in the several non-Pentecostal churches. For reasons I cannot detail here, Pentecostalism has not been a culture-shaping force and is not likely to become one in the foreseeable future, except as its social and political views are advanced by the fundamentalist-led religious new right.) Before looking ahead to possible developments, it is necessary to step back and ask how it happened that mainline Protestantism struck out, if indeed it has struck out.

### 'A Christian America'

One of the most influential religious books of recent years has been Sydney Ahlstrom's *A Religious History of the American People*. Ahlstrom's reading of American history puts Puritanism emphatically at the center of the story. This monumental study ends on a rather downbeat note: the mainline is dispirited and uncertain and, because he identifies American religion with the mainline, Ahlstrom suggests that we have entered a post-Christian era. Although Robert Handy is more modest in his inference, his *A Christian America* also and brilliantly depicts the decline of the Protestant establishment. Not only is that establishment unable to do what once it tried to do—now it does not even *want* to do what once it believed it had a divine mandate to do.

In the last few years, talk about a Christian America has been portrayed as an instance of right-wing extremism. But during most of our history it was as evident that America was Christian as that it was a republic. From the Mayflower Compact up through the social gospel that ended in this century, it was assumed that this is a Christian nation. The concern of the social gospel movement was simply that this Christian nation had not yet been thoroughly "Christianized." In the last century Horace Bushnell (d. 1876), a leading theological voice, articulated the assured consensus: "The wilderness shall bud and blossom as the rose before us; and we will not cease, till a christian nation throws up its temples of worship on every hill and plain; till knowledge, virtue and religion, blending, blending their dignity and their healthful power, have filled our great country with a manly and happy race of people, and the bands of a complete christian commonwealth are seen to span the continent" *(Barbarism the First Danger).*

In the nineteenth century all Protestants called themselves evangelicals, and there was no significant evangelical dissent from the vision Bushnell held forth. Nor was this vision limited to religious leaders. In 1892 the Supreme Court declared (*Church of the Holy Trinity* v. *U.S.*), "We are a Christian people, and the morality of the country is deeply ingrafted upon Christianity." As late as 1931 the same court could say without fear of contradiction: "We are a Christian people, according to one another the equal right of religious freedom, and acknowledging with reverence the duty of obedience to the will of God" (*U.S.* v. *Macintosh*). While the courts stopped using such language fifty years ago, it was commonplace in mainline Protestant pulpits and periodicals until twenty years ago.

When the religious new right emerged in 1978 and 1979, it too talked about a Christian America. Today it no longer does, at least not publicly. Its leaders have learned some lessons in pluralism from, among others, those people whose prayers God does hear after all. But, however clumsily, the Jerry Falwells were giving expression to something very deep in the American experience. It could be argued that this is not an instance of the circulation of elites; that it is not a case of a new group's picking up the language about Christian America after the old elite dropped it because they lost the nerve to assert it; that it is, rather, simply a matter of regression, of trying to go back to an era that is definitively past. That argument could be made, but I do not find it persuasive.

In the sense that a great majority of the population is Christian, this is a Christian nation. But for complex cultural and legal reasons, the statement that this is a Christian nation is now clearly too provocative. Yet what impulse or insight continues to tempt people to use the language of Christian America? It is, I believe, people's perception that democratic governance is not possible in defiance of the values of the people. They further perceive, correctly, that the core values of the American people are religiously based and, more specifically, based upon biblical, Judeo-Christian religion. Secularist mythologies to the contrary, the most serious questions a society must ask and answer cannot be resolved in a value-neutral manner. The most immediate evidence of this is the abortion debate and the failure of the Supreme Court to convince the American people of the resolution it proposed (in *Roe* v. *Wade*, 1973) to the question of who belongs to the human community and is entitled to legal protection.

In its more sanitized version, "Christian America" means that religiously based values cannot, because they are religiously based, be excluded from public deliberation, from the *agora* in which the business of the *polis* is conducted. It would seem at first that Jerry Falwell and Martin Luther King, Jr., have absolutely nothing in common. Certainly their analyses of the ills of America and the cures required could hardly be more different. But they are alike in this: both dared to intervene in the so-called secular realm, bringing down judgment and lifting up a vision of justice explicitly derived from biblical imperatives. Their interpretation of the biblical mandate is different, the policy content is different, but the process is the same. Both invoke biblical truth to provide moral legitimation and definition for the American experiment.

## Abandoning the Culture-Forming Task

In this respect Martin Luther King and Jerry Falwell stand in a venerable American tradition. In *Revivalism and Social Reform,* Timothy Smith demonstrates the ways in which an earlier mainline Protestantism joined religious passion and social change. Until the rise of the religious new right, even the current mainline insisted upon the inseparability of biblical truth from public justice. Only when The Moral Majority and others began to show that the rhetoric could be employed to quite different political ends did the mainline begin to develop scruples about mixing politics and religion. But, in fact, the mainline had much earlier abandoned the culture-forming tasks of Christianity.

This abandonment became evident in the theological self-understanding of the social gospel movement in the latter part of the nineteenth and the early part of this century. That might seem strange, for if Protestant Christianity was ever bullish on transforming American culture, surely it was during the era of the social gospel. Yet one must ask whether it was Christianity, with its transcendent truth claims, that was to transform society in the social gospel vision, or was it simply that Christian people and churches were to assist, maybe even to lead, in advancing that progress which was embraced and expected by "all men of good will"? The latter, I believe, was the case.

Washington Gladden, that great prophet of the social gospel movement, put it very revealingly: "The religions of the world are forced by the contacts and collisions of world politics into a struggle for existence; the evolutionary processes are sifting them; and we shall see the survival of the fittest—that religion which best meets the deepest needs of human nature." He was not in suspense about the outcome: "Doubtless each will make some contribution to that synthesis of faith which the ages are working out, but none of us doubts which one of them will stamp its character most strongly upon the final result."

Note that the issue is not the truth of Christianity but its fitness. And by what measure would Christianity be found the "fittest"? By its superior capacity to meet "the deepest needs of human nature." Those deepest needs, the context makes clear, are not reconciliation with God and life eternal but food, shelter, education, freedom from terror, and a secure place in a society of equality and peace. Transcendent hope had been replaced by the Great Society. Such a Christianity could no longer shape culture because it had been thoroughly assimilated into the culture's vision of its own happy and inevitable future.

I do not suggest that the earlier union of revivalism and reform described by Timothy Smith was completely sundered. Far from it. At the heart of the social gospel movement and at the heart of mainline liberal activism today can be found people of profound spirituality and theological astuteness. But a fundamental change had taken place in the self-understanding of mainline Protestantism. At first it was subtle. Many decades would pass before it erupted in the more vulgar form of the World Council of Churches' pronouncement that "the world sets the agenda for the church."

## Conforming, Not Transforming

The social gospel movement was devoted to many unexceptionable, indeed laudable, goals. But with the social gospel movement, establishment Protestantism assumed an ancillary and supportive posture toward the culture. The direction of the culture could not be brought under divine judgment because the culture itself was seen as the working out of God's purposes in history. To borrow Pauline terminology from Romans 12, the Church's mission was no longer to transform the culture but to be conformed to a culture that was transforming itself into the heavenly kingdom.

Some historians have called the religious era from 1870 to 1920 the "third great awakening." According to them it was the time when American religion came of age in daringly relating itself to the modern world. But I believe Robert Handy is closer to the truth in describing that era as the "second disestablishment." The first disestablishment had happened by the early nineteenth century, when there were no longer established churches in the several states. It ushered in an era of voluntaristic vitality and growth. The second disestablishment was more ominous. The restive truth claims were tamed and the rough edges of transcendent judgment were smoothed as Protestantism accommodated itself to, indeed exulted in, its cultural captivity.

J. Gresham Machen and other less impressive souls dissented from this accommodation. But the fundamentalism to which they gave birth provided no compelling alternative vision. It seemed reactive and sour. Its resounding No to modernity seemed as sterile, as bereft of culture-transforming power, as did liberalism's accommodating Yes. By the end of the 1920s, fundamentalism with all its works and all its ways had been expelled from the circles of the influential and respectable. In truth, fundamentalism retreated almost faster than it could be expelled. Aside from occasional forays, it would not be heard from again for more than forty years. The mainline was left in secure possession of all the religious turf that mattered, or so the mainline thought.

In exile, fundamentalism licked its wounds and nurtured its grudges. But it also busily set about building an alternative "righteous empire," to use Martin Marty's phrase. It had lost touch with the elite but not with millions of believers. Following World War II the mainline became uneasily aware that there was another world out there. The stirrings became, quite unmistakably, a movement. Soon the "fundies" had colleges that were impertinent enough to apply for accreditation. There were fundamentalists with Ph.D.s who called for dialogue in place of derision. And these folks seemed to have a knack for the technologies of communication with all kinds of people who had shown little interest in mainline Protestantism.

The first fundamentalists to return from exile called themselves "neo-evangelicals." They were very civil and very impressive. Then the "neo" was dropped, and some of the pushier types started to come back. Before long, 1976 to be precise, they had the gall to acclaim "The Year of the Evangelicals." It was too late to shut the door now. By 1979 the noisiest and most aggressive types had arrived, announcing themselves as The Moral Majority. They even called themselves fundamentalists—right out, just like that. And that is when the mainline Protestants began to wonder whether *they* were not in exile.

But we get ahead of ourselves. By the mid-1930s a terrible thing had happened to the mainline social witness: it had succeeded. With the arrival of the New Deal, the basic direction was set that was supposed to lead to the rule of heaven on earth. The New Deal did not establish the "socialism of Christian equality and love" that social gospelers had called for, but it presumably put America on the road to that happy goal. The crucial "turning around of America" (to use the favored phrase of today's religious new right) had been achieved.

As it turned out, the decades to follow were to be disappointing to socially concerned Protestants. First there was World War II. Later there was the exhilarating period of the early civil rights movement under the leadership of Dr. Martin Luther King, Jr., which was able to get legally mandated segregation struck down but did not produce a racially integrated or equal society. The last great spurt of domestic innovation in the New Deal tradition came with Lyndon Johnson's Great Society programs. Far from reviving liberal confidence, however, that collapsed in a cacophony of re-crimination over Vietnam and what began to be perceived as the "systemic" evils of the American social, economic, and political system. In this view, the injustice America practiced at home was matched in evil only by the oppression it practiced abroad.

## Warnings From 'Christian Realism'

Liberal Protestantism is a very long way from the confidence, even euphoria, that marked its social witness from the late nineteenth century through the 1920s. Along the way there were voices warning against this identification of Christian truth with cultural trends. Most notably there were the Brothers Niebuhr. H. Richard brilliantly exposed the facile assumptions that under-lay the wedding between social progress and ideas about the King-dom of God in American life. Reinhold thundered elegantly in opposition to the pacifism that had become an integral part of liberal Protestant thought. In the face of Hitler's threat, and in sympathy with the "crisis theology" of the Continent, he articulated a position of "Christian realism," calling for a daringly modest exercise of responsibility in a radically imperfect world.

Niebuhr seemed to carry the day. Generally speaking, mainline Protestantism rallied to the flag in World War II. And if it did not exactly rally to the flag during the Korean War, neither did it burn the flag. But one may ask whether, during the crusade against Nazism, the mainline internalized Niebuhr's critique or once again merely accommodated itself to the line of march set by American liberalism and led by FDR. The argument could be made that current mainline sympathy for the necessity of violence in Third World "liberation struggles" is—in an ironic way that Reinhold Niebuhr would appreciate—a curious form of "Christian realism." In passages of *The Irony of American History* (1952) Niebuhr wrote with great prescience about how leaders of new and poor nations would undermine the morale of the Western democracies by exploiting their sense of guilt about their prosperity and power. Some church-and-society offices of mainline Protestantism today eagerly join in that process of exploitation.

It is again ironic that in the past decade, when Reinhold Niebuhr's understanding of America's role in world history has been thoroughly expunged from mainline thinking, the cross street by 475 Riverside has been renamed Reinhold Niebuhr Drive. His and his brother's warnings against the marriage between transcendent truth and historical trends have been largely ignored. Mainline Protestantism rode what was thought to be the tide of the future and now looks like the backwater. In the bitterness of its isolation, its pronouncements become more acerb; in its disappointment and anger at being betrayed by the America it had wed, establishment Protestantism becomes ever more "prophetic," which is small consolation for being ignored.

Shortly before the 1980 elections, *engage/social action,* a United Methodist magazine, criticized the religious new right for suggesting that there is a Christian position on a host of public issues. In the same issue the editors offered a column-by-column comparison of the Democratic, Republican, and Anderson platforms with

the "official positions" of the United Methodist Church. On issue
after issue—from defense policy to affirmative action to abortion—the church's official positions were those of the Democratic
party. Where there were differences, they would have been resolved had the McGovern-Kennedy wing of the party prevailed in
writing the platform. What is true of the Methodists is, with few
exceptions, true of the United Presbyterians, the Episcopalians,
the United Church of Christ, and others. On all these issues they
may be right and their opponents wrong. But the inescapable fact is
that they have invested the fortunes of their self-described "constituency of conscience" in a political past that may be an ineffectual
minority for years to come.

Five basic themes marked the old Democratic majority and have
now been captured by conservative Republicanism: a strong and
anti-Communist foreign policy; a commitment to economic
growth as the surest way to domestic justice; a devotion to eradicat-
ing discrimination and opposition to quotas in all forms; a populist
respect for the values of ordinary Americans; and a vision of
America as a compassionate and caring society. Except for the last,
the new majority, now Republican, has preempted these themes of
an older liberalism. Thus the case could be made that mainline
Protestantism has not been abandoned by the older liberalism to
which it was once devoted. Rather, it might be argued, mainline
Protestantism and other sectors of "radicalized" liberalism in the
convulsions of the sixties and seventies surrendered the core
themes of the older liberalism to the leaders of the new conservative majority. This is an analysis favored by older liberals, now
called neo-conservatives, to whom it is important to believe that it
is not *they* who have changed. It is a persuasive, if not entirely
convincing, argument.

### 'Is America a Force For Good?'

What I do find convincing is the proposition that much of the
leadership of mainline Protestantism cannot contribute to the
moral legitimation and definition of the American experiment
because, when all is said and done, it no longer believes in that

experiment. In admittedly unscientific research, I have asked scores of mainline Protestant leaders what the response would be if a certain question were put to the middle and upper management at 475 Riverside Drive and at various denominational headquarters. The question is this: On balance, and considering the alternatives, is America a force for good in the world? Informed estimates suggest that no more than 10 or 15 per cent of mainline leadership would readily answer that question in the affirmative. The great majority either would add so many equivocations as to make their answer tantamount to negative, or would baldly state that America is a force for evil.

Is the question simplistic? I think not. Not in the larger view of our world historical moment. In the alignments of power and influence, there is on one side the United States, its Western European allies, and Japan. On the other side are the Soviet Union and its for the most part unwilling allies. Then there are all the other countries, constituting not so much a third contending force as a clustering of diverse interests and needs, of people who are variously ignored or contended for by the two dominant factions, depending upon their resources or strategic importance. Given the chief contention between Soviet and American blocs, it is not simplistic to ask whether the success of one or of the other would be better for the future of humankind.

Of course, one can invoke a curse upon both their houses and declare oneself on the side of those who are outside or marginal to the contention. Choosing that option, however, just as surely removes one from any role in redefining America. The American people are not likely to accept their directions from those who have invoked a curse upon America, even if the curse is applied to America's chief rival with equal sincerity. Martin Luther King was fond of saying, "Whom you would change you must first love." This is not the same as the reactionary slogan of the sixties, "Love it or leave it." Love, because it is love, must often be critical. Certainly Dr. King was harshly critical. But his "dream" was a dream *for* America, not against it. Similarly, Walter Rauschenbusch, Washington Gladden, Lyman Abbot, and other leaders of the social gospel movement were critical, but they did not doubt that, in the short and long run, America's influence was not only good for the world but the hope of the world.

This, I believe, is the story line in understanding the present situation of mainline Protestantism: For two centuries it provided a transcendent vision of the American possibility; in the social gospel movement it proposed wedding that vision to a very immanent program of social reform; in New Deal liberalism that marriage was consummated; amid the departure of New Deal confidence and the arrival of assassinations, Vietnam, and riotous discontent, the marriage was terminated.

Although now the heirs of Puritanism sulk in the bitter aftereffects of divorce, it is well to remember that the story, because it is a story, is not yet over. Mainline leadership could make a dramatic change of direction, in line with the winds of cultural and political change. Or the leadership could be replaced in a revolt by the constituencies with which that leadership is largely out of touch. But there is little evidence at hand for either prospect. For the foreseeable future, mainline Protestantism will not be a major player in redefining and reconstructing the American experiment.

With apologies to Spinoza: transcendence abhors a vacuum. Every society needs some transcendent referent that is the source of its sanctions, legitimacy, and direction. Otherwise it is simply a society adrift. Because Americans are, for better and for worse, an exceedingly religious people, that transcendent referent must be carried and shaped by religion. Now the most aggressive force moving, indeed leaping, into the vacuum is the religious new right. As long as other religious candidates hold back or disdain the culture-forming tasks, the religious new right will seize the attention and grow in influence. I do not expect, however, that Moral Majority and its allies will have the field to themselves for long. I hope not. The religious new right is not up to the task that must be undertaken.

That task is—to state a monumentally complex thesis very briefly—to reconstruct Western public philosophy after the collapse of the two-hundred-year-old hegemony of the secular enlightenment. We are witnessing that collapse in every sphere—the sciences, the arts, law, political philosophy. Social scientists who twenty and even ten years ago assumed a necessary connection between modernity and secularization have now made a dramatic reversal. Surveying the exhaustion of secularistic philosophies, thinkers such as Daniel Bell and Robert Nisbet look, somewhat wanly, for hope in a religious renascence. It is noteworthy that the leadership of American Jewry is no longer so certain that it is good for Jews and other minorities to live in a secularized society in which there is no absolute prohibition against evil, including the evil of anti-Semitism.

There is a growing recognition that individual and communal rights are treacherously insecure unless grounded in the deepest—that is to say, religious—beliefs of a people. The great threat to pluralism is not militant religion but the static power of religionless utilitarianism and majoritarianism. The question posed by this watershed moment in the American experiment is, In what sense are we and in what sense are we not a secular society? Though his language is foreign to us, Horace Bushnell's intuition about "a compleat christian commonwealth" is irrepressible.

## Candidates For the Culture-Forming Role

Finally, we return to the potential candidates who might help answer such questions of culture-informing and culture-transforming moment. There is the religious new right. In the default of others, it will continue to exercise great influence, for bad and for good. Its fundamentalist religious base offers very little in conceptual resources or sophistication. Its pre-millennialistic and apocalyptic view of history is in inevitable conflict with a vision of world-historical hope and is implausible to those who do not subscribe to its peculiar reading of scriptural prophecy. It does have, thanks to its communications technology and its alliance with the political new right, a formidable advantage in organizing electoral victories and defeats. And Jerry Falwell is correct, I believe, in stating that "on most of our issues most of the American people agree with us." Agreeing on some or even most of the issues, however, is not the same thing as liking The Moral Majority or accepting its leadership.

Then there are the Roman Catholics. They have the numbers to take the lead in relating Christian witness to public policy. Indeed, Catholics were a crucial ingredient in the political triumph of the New Deal. But until Vatican II and the election of John F. Kennedy—and perhaps still today—Catholics were uneasy about their relationship to the American experiment. That uneasiness was exacerbated by anti-Catholicism in a country that habitually equated Christianity with Protestantism. Conceptually, Roman Catholics have a rich tradition of theoretical and practical reflection, ranging from Thomas Aquinas through John Courtney Murray. Being central to the pro-life side of the abortion debate, they have a strong hold on the single most important question connecting public policy with religious based values. In the Pope they have an articulate center of teaching without equal or even serious competition in the world.

But is the leadership of American Catholicism—episcopal, theological, and social—out of touch with its own tradition and its own constituency? This too would be irony, if the Catholic leadership, so eager to be "Americanized," has emulated mainline Protestantism to the extent that it too has struck out, but before it ever got a proper turn at bat. A comparison of the public positions on both foreign and domestic issues of the National Conference of Catholic Bishops with those of the National Council of Churches is not encouraging. And it is best not even to mention the captivity of influential religious orders and other organizations to the "liberationist" mentality, which—whatever its merits—disqualifies them from taking part in the redefining of America.

The Lutheran tradition is not conceptually strong regarding the Christian tasks in culture. Whether German or Scandinavian, a two-kingdoms theology and an authoritarian mentality are of little help in providing a religious rationale for democratic governance. There is in American Lutheranism, however, a sense of newness, even of strangeness, that has largely immunized it from the dead-ended mainline consensus. There is a strong awareness of transcendence by which this and all social orders can be kept under judgment. And there are in my experience many Lutheran thinkers who have moved beyond the limitations of their tradition.

THE POST-SECULAR TASK OF THE CHURCHES    17

Finally, there are millions of Lutherans who are basically sympathetic to the themes around which a new American majority is building. Yet Lutheranism, which fifteen years ago was called by Winthrop Hudson "the sleeping giant" of American religion, for the most part sleeps on.

And so, at last, back to the evangelicals. That is a vast, diverse world, spread from the fundamentalism of the religious new right to the liberationism on the other side of 475 Riverside. It includes groups like the *Sojourners* community, politically indistinguishable from the radicalized left, except on abortion (and that ever so lately). It includes, stretching the category a bit, the biblically grounded radicalism of John Howard Yoder and his "politics of Jesus." It also includes a few million who would be surprised to be told that they differ at all from the theology (so to speak) or the politics of Jerry Falwell or even Bob Jones. Evangelicalism's conceptual history, largely forgotten by most evangelicals, is rooted in the sundry enthusiasms of the "radical" Reformation. Aside from Roger Williams, whom it is respectable to invoke on public questions, the political side of that heritage has been safely domesticated by the evangelical sojourn in America. A "strict separationism" between church and state still inhibits some Baptists and others from mixing it up in the public arena. But one suspects that those separationist passions, historically fired in large part by anti-Catholicism, will increasingly be dampened.

The real Calvinists are usually included in the evangelical sector. They are small in number but strong in a tradition that, perhaps a few centuries before its time, tried to work out an alternative to the medieval structure of society. Perhaps history had to experience another alternative, that of the secular Enlightenment, and learn from it and in many ways gain from it, before we would be prepared to ponder again the first-principle questions posed by the great reformer of Geneva. As I said before, among those who today are seriously thinking through the meaning of—and the alternatives to—a secular society, I am impressed by how many call themselves Calvinists.

Thus we are left with a ragtag band of believers who have come upon a historical moment for which we are not prepared. There are moral crusaders who may be doing some good things and some bad things but have not thought very seriously about just what it is they are doing; they may not know much about theology or political philososphy, but they know what they don't like. There are others who have been at this business of culture-formation for a long time, but now they no longer have the stomach for it. Then there are others, perhaps the majority, who are surprised, perhaps pleased, and a little embarrassed to be told that it may be up to them.

In this drama of relating Christian faith and public life, the old actors are exhausted and the new ones are impossible. Post-secular America has a religious role in search of religious leadership that has the nerve for it.

# The Changing Catholic Scene

JAMES V. SCHALL, S.J.

IN 1960 FLANNERY O'CONNOR WROTE a short note to Roslyn Barnes in which she recalled her studies at the University of Iowa. The question arose whether Miss O'Connor had ever met Monsignor Conway, a chaplain at the university and the author of a widely used catechism called *Questions Catholics Are Asked.* Flannery O'Connor could not recall having met the priest, though she had attended Mass almost daily at nearby St. Mary's Parish. She wrote, "I went there three years and never knew a soul in that congregation or any of the priests, but it was not necessary. As soon as I went in the door, I was at home. . . ."[1]

On hearing such a comment, many a contemporary Christian would throw up his hands in horror. Yet Flannery O'Connor, a good Christian, far from complaining, was pointing out the true purpose of going to church, a purpose that transcends social and political concerns. We go to church because it is our spiritual home, because what we find and do there cannot be found and done elsewhere. This will be the background theme I shall pursue in my reflections on the social thinking of modern Catholicism. Religion has to do with transcendence, and this higher reality is essential to

*James V. Schall, S.J., is an associate professor of government at Georgetown University, Washington, D.C. He is a consultor to the Pontifical Commission on Justice and Peace. Among his books are "Christianity and Politics," "Christianity and Life," "Far Too Easily Pleased: A Theology of Contemplation, Play, and Festivity," and (forthcoming) "Liberation Theology."*

us, no matter what socio-economic or cultural environment we live in, no matter what our theories on the practical public order.

To approach the subject from a different angle, social philosophy ought to be based on the priority of a person's relation to the transcendent God. The former exists for the latter, the person for God, not vice versa. If a real relationship exists, the transcendent will necessarily affect our public and private lives.

In 1954, Professor Heinrich Rommen, writing about the Church and human rights, said:

> First Christianity is intrinsically universal; it is ordained for mankind, the community of nations, not to a particular state only; it is above nation-states, national cultures, and civilizations. And its purpose is not "secular" or transitory, but perpetual, to be performed within all historical cultures whether favorable, indifferent, or unfavorable. Its purpose is the salvation of individual souls, however much they may be immersed in their specific cultural patterns and historicity.[2]

Personal dignity in whatever culture is grounded in each person's uniqueness, which transcends the particular shape of the culture. Christianity cannot in principle embrace any form of cultural relativism that would make men essentially differ from one another simply on the basis of culture.[3] Culture is a way of being more ourselves, an expression of what we do with our freedom, but it never exhausts or defines all of what we are.[4] Christianity teaches that there is something given in us, to us, that transcends the world itself. The sense of personal transcendence in whatever place or era, whether by a Flannery O'Connor alone at Mass or a Heinrich Rommen ruminating on personal salvation, incites human beings to accomplish what they can on earth.

Whenever men seek personal salvation in a God who transcends historical life—an unpopular doctrine today as it denies the implied absolutism of the socio-economic order—they prevent the corruption of politics by the divine and of the divine by politics. Historically, the symbolic affirmation of this point, at least in the Catholic Church, has been the principle that the clergy had a function that needed no justification in political, social, economic, or artistic terms. Currently, however, unless a priest "does" something socially relevant, he is thought to have no contribution to make to "society." In his February 1981 Address to Men Religious in the Manila Cathedral, Pope John Paul II restored the perspective tellingly:

> At the same time I ask you to observe this guideline: that each apostolic endeavor should be in harmony with the teaching of the Church, with the apostolic purposes of your individual institutes. May I also remind you of my words at Guadalupe: "You are priests and religious; you are not social or political leaders or officials of a temporal power. . . . Let us not be under the illusion that we are serving the Gospel if we 'dilute' our charism through an exaggerated interest in the wide field of temporal problems." It is important for people to see you as "servants of Christ and stewards of the mysteries of God."[5]

John Paul II's characteristic teaching on temporal matters is that they are properly in the competence of lay men and women. They need not be seen from the perspective of modern ideology. Rather they can be illuminated by the resources and traditions of Christianity. The Pope said at Puebla:

> Let us keep in mind that the Church's action in earthly matters such as human advancement, development, justice, the rights of the individual, is always intended to be at the service of man; and of man as she sees him in the Christian vision of the anthropology that she adopts. She therefore does not need to have recourse to ideological systems in order to love, defend, and collaborate in the liberation of man. . . .[6]

Christians would suspect, therefore, that we are unlikely to be right about society if we are not right about what transcends it, even though politics belongs to the natural order and faith has no specific social program.

## Modern Political Theory—Away From 'Ought'

Political philosophers distinguish between what men *do* and what they *ought* to do. But Machiavelli remarked that the essential political error was to aim too high, that politics was corrupted by religion and metaphysics.[7] Political science should be aimed at what we can *expect* men to do, not at what they ought to do. And if we are wise, we will expect men to do some pretty dreary, not to say shocking, things. The "wild beast within us" of which Plato spoke in the ninth book of *The Republic* is a rather accurate description of what can happen. Not to expect and account for the worst is to forgo any political realism.

This shift from the "ought" of classical and medieval theory is the foundation of modern political theory. Machiavelli, its acknowledged founder, seems at first sight to be a sort of St. Augustine without the consolation of the City of God. But it is one thing to look upon human evil and suffering from the perspective of an eternal life and quite another to suggest that this earthly life is all there is. Augustine, though aware of all the baseness of human nature that Machiavelli was to depict, had the advantage of a theological reason to account for it, and, further, followed Plato in taking seriously man's quest for ideal perfection. Augustine sought to discover the proper location of the City of God. He held that it was not merely in the mind, nor was it in any earthly city or experience. But unlike Machiavelli, who gave up and accepted evil as a legitimate political tool, Augustine held that the true City of God did exist and that to seek it was the most important task we could undertake.[8]

The abiding importance of Augustine's political thought, however, is that he intellectually prevented Christians from making the establishment of a City of God on earth the prime political goal open to man. Although Augustine understood that politics and religion were not the same thing, he Christianized Plato's thinking, establishing a link between philosophy and the City by recognizing that in any community, people long for an end that satisfies them absolutely—what Augustine came to call "peace."

The Augustinian and Machiavellian realist traditions, however, held in common a vivid sense of the irregularity, corruption, and even perverseness of earthly and human things. Politics was substantially remedial, designed to reorder what had gotten out of hand. Coercion existed and was to be used, even though it "ought not" to exist, since man was created good.

Machiavelli simplified the problem by assigning evil to human nature as such. Augustine, however, located the origin of evil not in our created nature or in our institutions but in our wills.[9] Man is good, but he can and does choose contrary to his own nature and well-being. In the Judeo-Christian understanding of things, to choose evil is ultimately to choose against oneself.

Given our imperfect human reality, the state became at the least necessary. It appeared on the human scene as a punisher and regulator of the disorders arising from the human will. St. Paul told the Romans of his time, in words we do not particularly relish:

> Since all government comes from God, the civil authorities were appointed by God, and so anyone who resists authority is rebelling against God's decision, and such an act is bound to be punished. Good behavior is not afraid of magistrates; only criminals have anything to fear. . . . The state is there to serve God for your benefit. If you break the law, however, you may well have to fear: the bearing of the sword has its significance. The authorities are there to serve God: they carry out God's revenge by punishing wrongdoers. You are afraid of being punished, but also for conscience' sake.[10]

And as if this were not enough, Paul went on to suggest that "this is the reason you must pay taxes. . . ." The sword, taxes, and punishment all find their justification here. Neither Paul nor Augustine is likely to deceive men with claims that a sinless or perfect order is around the corner or down the ages.

## Christian Tradition and the Heavenly City

Augustine's realism contrasted with the Aristotelian-Thomistic notion, which had to account for the same facts of actual human experience. Although Aquinas did not in any sense deny what Augustine had taught about politics, he did place it in a higher order.

There was still, however, no escaping the evidence that something was radically wrong. In the late Middle Ages and on into the modern period, a belief developed that perhaps the disorder could be removed by a more optimistic, this-worldly theory that could identify and remove the problem by political means. This endeavor lies at the heart of current religious problems with politics.

Chesterton remarked that original sin is the one Christian

dogma that needs no special proof, since all we need do is go out in the streets and open our eyes. In the central Thomist tradition, political and economic institutions are good and essential elements of human life. There can nevertheless be good or bad, better or worse, forms of government or economy.

For Aquinas, though revelation has a remedial and illuminating effect on politics and economics, the source of political and economic knowledge is not Scripture or faith. The reason why men and women belong to a polity is the reverse, almost, of why they belong to a religion. Aquinas tells us that religion and nature are ultimately compatible, and this implies, of course, that they are not the same thing.

The easily observable fact that many things went wrong did not necessarily mean that "the things of Caesar" were not to be observed. The original element in Christ's announced dichotomy between Caesar's and God's things was the religious affirmation that Caesar *did* have a legitimate terrain that religion must respect. The striking contribution of Christianity to political theory was the liberation of politics to be itself and not merely a subdivision of religion in an enclosed system. Politics was limited, but its limitation did not make it evil or corrupt. In classical metaphysics, something can be limited and still good.

Aristotle's affirmation that politics had a proper autonomy and legitimacy was also grounded in Christian thought. But just as religion ought not to control politics, so politics ought not to proceed as if religion did not exist. Religion's claim of a transcendent status was the beginning of the theory of the limited state and constitutionalism that has characterized Western history.[11] The first political freedom, then, was that of placing limits upon politics, which was possible only when politics knew why it was limited in the first place. The last political temptation, on the other hand, as the Book of Revelation intimated, was that politics was more than itself, that it was indeed everything.

Religion has been called "the opiate of the people." Paradoxically, in some trends in social and political thinking in the Catholic Church today, "the people" in the abstract have become the opiate of religion. Marx's contention that religion distracted men from their earthly tasks has provoked an extreme reaction—that religion should address men only in political terms. The tenor of our times in discussing religion and politics is to force religion to justify itself, even to think about itself in socio-economic terms, which often it seems quite willing to do. This phenomenon is what John Paul II calls "reductionism," the selection of a framework or model that by its very form excludes the religious reality.[12]

If we are to understand the particularly Catholic varieties of social thought, we must recognize that a sort of "Christendom of the Left" has supplanted the so-called Christendom of the Right. The intellectual problem involved is not so new or significant as the question of why this reversal occurred.

The attempt to locate the change in political emphasis has obscured the fact that almost for the first time in modern history, a socio-economic-political theory originating in classical Judeo-Christian theory and dogma is possible. The groundwork has been laid in the history of science, in the relation of science to theology, in the fact that systematic science was spawned in the theories of creation, law, essence, and intellect, the latter capable of knowing "being," of knowing something outside itself.[13] The only thing that will prevent us from realizing the theoretical impact of the relation of science and classic theology to political and social theory will be a sort of breach of trust that will keep Christian social thinking mired in its efforts to politicize religion and constrict it into a closed ideology.

In a passage in *The Heavenly City of the Eighteenth Century Philosophers*, Carl Becker, writing in 1931, anticipated that the main challenge to religion in the twentieth century would come precisely from the ideological attempt to relocate the City of God to earth.[14] The Enlightenment effort to domesticate and secularize Christian salvation history was revived by men of our century, despite two world wars and the theories of the City of the Damned on Earth and the Decline of the West that they spawned. Becker wrote:

> The Garden of Eden was for [the *Philosophes*, the leaders of the eighteenth-century French Enlightenment] a myth, no doubt, but they looked enviously both to the Golden Age of Roman

virtue, and across the waters to the unspoiled innocence of an Arcadian civilization that flourished in Pennsylvania. . . . They courageously discussed atheism, but not before the servants. They defended toleration valiantly, but could with difficulty tolerate priests. They denied that miracles ever happened, but they believed in the perfectibility of the human race. . . . [Thus] I shall attempt to show that the *Philosophes* demolished the Heavenly City of Augustine only to rebuild it with more up-to-date materials.[15]

Becker wrote in the midst of the Depression, in the same year that saw Pius XI's *Quadragesimo Anno*. The pertinence of his book has increased steadily, for the eighteenth-century Philosophes have evolved into the late twentieth-century clerics.[16] Just as the worldly philosopher followed the Christian outline in an imitative manner, so our presumably other-worldly cleric adopts the enthusiasm of the ideologue.

It is difficult to sort all this out without giving some attention to the modern history of Catholicism. This year marks the ninetieth anniversary of Leo XIII's famous encyclical "On the Condition of the Working Classes" (May 15, 1891), which is generally credited with the growth of specifically Catholic social thought, and it seems appropriate to begin with this statement.

Leo's encyclical, *Rerum Novarum*, and those published on its anniversary—*Quadragesimo Anno* in 1931, *Mater et Magistra* in 1961, *Octagesima Adveniens* in 1971, and *Laborem Exercens* in 1981—are a part of the considerable body of official statements of the Roman See on political, social, and economic questions, though this tradition itself disclaims any direct competence in economic or political matters. The fact that such an authoritative body of teaching exists makes the Catholic Church different from all other religious bodies. Constant efforts to "reinterpret" the body of teaching according to various ideological designs or genuinely new knowledge make it appear less stable than it actually is.

The Catholic social experience, of course, did not begin in the nineteenth century when Germany and Italy became nation-states at the expense of the Papal States. It had already existed for a thousand years, an incomprehensible thought to many of our contemporaries. But it was in the last century that Napoleon and Bismarck established compromises and conditions concerning the public place of the Church in modern European society. The relation between a "democracy" and a "church" was a central issue in the nineteenth century. Various theories of democracy seemed absolutist to the Church, and often in fact were, while the Church seemed an enemy to the European democracies. It was mostly Bismarck who taught the Church the value of the democratic process, while Napoleon taught the revolution that it could never eradicate the faith.[17]

## The French Revolution — Against Poverty

It is important to recall, however, the vast disarray of the French Revolution that preceded Napoleon. As Hannah Arendt pointed out, unless we understand the French Revolution, we will not comprehend twentieth-century revolutionary thought, which holds that an authentic revolution must follow the French model rather than the American counterpart.[18]

The essence of the French model concerned the relation of the poor to the revolution. Poverty, not freedom, was its moral justification, and ever since we have had the confused thought that to rid ourselves of poverty we must also rid ourselves of freedom. In America the poor were free and independent, whereas in France the poor were miserable and helpless—unable to better their lot without mass uprisings. Poverty was a product of oppression and could be alleviated only by revolution.

This strange background is, I believe, at the heart of the growing division within the churches over the problem of poverty. For some, the poor, identified with "the people" and thoroughly undistinguished by individual characteristics, are used to justify a "necessary" political "option"—a socialist form of government. Despite recurrent failures of socialist systems, this option is still embraced for abstract, ideological reasons. Any effort to alleviate poverty through innovative freedom and responsible free exchange is rejected in the name of an ideology modeled ultimately on the French Revolution.

On the economic front, the Industrial Revolution had a great impact on Catholic thinking. The central point of inquiry, however, is why it came so late in the Catholic countries. The intellectual analysis of this tardiness has in our century been applied to the Third World, or the developing countries, which have replaced Catholic Latin Europe as the "backward" area in need of structural reform.

Lenin's *Imperialism* was elemental in this respect, for in his efforts to save Marxism from itself, Lenin shifted the exploited of the earth—the "working classes" or proletariat—from Europe to the old colonial empires. In this sense, there is a relation between Marxism's efforts to save itself from the intellectual disaster of a contradicted historical theory and Latin Catholicism's efforts to defend itself against the charge of backwardness by the Protestant ethic. It is evidently no accident that the neo-Confucian economies of East Asia based on the model from the north of Europe are currently the most productive in the world, while intellectuals in the Catholic Latin cultures with their overseas cultural extensions are the only ones who do not seem to know that Marxism is dead. Are we facing the irony of seeing religion—the Catholic religion, of all things—become the savior of Marxism?

I used to teach in Rome, and each year I read several books on economic history with my students, who were largely clerics from the Third World. The book that invariably received hushed attention was Max Weber's *The Protestant Ethic and the Spirit of Capitalism*. Over the years I developed a theory about this. I decided that the Weber thesis, however much it has been analyzed from a Catholic viewpoint, is related to the religious revolutionary drive to stigmatize capitalism as the root of all social evils, especially in the Third World. This theory led me to postulate the counterthesis that "anti-capitalism" is the major cause of underdevelopment, that religion is fast becoming the major promoter of this "anti-capitalist" underdevelopment, and that people like Julius Nyerere, for all their religious good will, choose ideological models that make it impossible for their people to escape poverty.

To reject capitalism on spiritual grounds was not, in fact, Weber's intention. He attacked the economic determinism of

Marx. Contrary to Marx, Weber endeavored to establish that spiritual changes cause economic changes.

I view the current liberation theology movement (including its German intellectual origins) as a kind of southern European, Latin American revenge on Protestantism. Though it is done in the name of Catholicism, the form is Marxist, which enables activist Protestants and Catholics to join in a Marxist analysis over against the successful modes of development. This also explains why Japan and neo-Confucian countries are not admitted to the discourse, since they have developed successfully through neo-capitalistic endeavors.

There are no doubt too many paradoxes here, even for a distant follower of Chesterton like myself. Yet I think there is more than a little truth in the argument, which helps explain why religion has become so politicized.[19]

## Varieties of Catholic Political Thought

There is something subtly dangerous in attempting to describe the Catholic left, center, and right, for in the light of what I have suggested above, to analyze religion in political or economic terms leaves aside most of what religion should be about. Moreover, we currently have a Pope who has repeatedly insisted that religion is the first and foremost *human* right.[20] This is the first political consequence of Christian transcendence.

Yet we Christians are often sadly unconcerned about genuine religious freedom, particularly in Marxist states. What solicitude we do show is ideologically tainted. Czechoslovakia evokes indifference; Vietnam is forgotten. Religious freedom for Christians and would-be Christians in Muslim states is at best minimal. Christian missionaries are welcome in India mostly as school teachers or nurses. The Church is dying in a Cuba hailed as the model of much religious revolutionary theory.[21]

Unlike the Jews in Russia, who seem at least to consider leaving an oppressive country, the Christian is more often told he ought to stay. And if he should decide he wants to leave, little church assistance is available to him. For ever since Augustine, the Christian has claimed to be an exemplary citizen, whatever the circumstances. There has been a strong pressure within Christianity to remain when the structures of society politically or religiously close against religious people. After Mao Tse-tung's takeover in China in 1948, for instance, Catholic priests were told to stay until expelled, or worse. (Many of those expelled lived to see Mao exalted by Catholics in the 1970s as the builder of a kind of natural Christian society without Christianity.[22])

Christians believe in the value of suffering injustice as well as in the inner freedom of the oppressor, who by grace or choice might eventually change his mind and heart. The right to self-defense, the just war, even tyrannicide in special cases are not denied by Catholic tradition. But not everything is permitted. Religious Machiavellianism, for example, is a contradiction in terms.[23]

One aspect of Catholic thinking about the public order has to do with the freedom of the Church simply to survive, to preach, to teach, to administer the sacraments. This activity is not considered to be "against" any state: it lies in a realm not under the legitimate competence of the state. The ability to know and to adhere to what is essential has been decisive to the survival of Christians in absolutist societies.

In the Catholic social encyclicals, especially the early ones, there was a vivid sense that the modern economic, political, and social world was founded against a more wholesome medieval Christian experience. There is a distinct relation between this and the intellectual controversy surrounding classical and modern political theory. Leo XIII, for instance, wrote in *Rerum Novarum*:

> The ancient workingmen's guilds were destroyed in the past century, and no other organization took their place. Public institutions and the laws have repudiated the ancient religion. Hence, by degree it has come to pass that working men have been given over, isolated and defenseless, to the callousness of employers and the greed of unrestrained competition [#2].

Nostalgia for the past was long considered a sign that the Church rejected the modern world. Indeed, one of the main causes of the enthusiasm for Pope John XXIII was the assumption that he had come to terms with modern political and economic institutions.

But as it happened, the world was then on the point of rejecting many of these same institutions. In consequence, people like John Courtney Murray and Jacques Maritain, architects of the rationale for a modern Catholicism, were often repudiated as conservatives.[24] The reason, of course, was that separation of religion and politics, for which these thinkers had striven, was no longer an ideal of the Christian left. Religion became useful as a tool to foster the revolutionary project, so that, in effect, the reunion of throne and altar reappeared in a peculiar political fashion.

Meanwhile, in its political thinking the Church came to recognize that republican democracy was not merely legitimate but the better form of polity. The political struggle of Catholicism with the modern world extended from the Reformation through such episodes as the American First Amendment, the Belgian separation from Holland, the adept politics of the German Center party during Bismarck's troubles with the socialists, Don Luigi Sturzo's Italian Popolare party, the sobering experiences under Fascism and Nazism, the Christian Democratic parties, and Vatican II. Particularly significant were Pius XII's Christmas Addresses on Democracy and John XXIII's *Pacem in Terris*, perhaps the best statement on political structures ever to come from a corporate body, religious or secular.

Up until World War II, indeed almost up until John XXIII and Paul VI, Catholic social documents were written within the context of the Industrial Revolution and its consequences. Invariably, they analyzed the liberal and socialist extremes and attempted to locate the Catholic position somewhere in the middle. I recall in the 1970s in Italy several essays from the so-called Christian left suggesting that the Catholic Church had no political or social thought of its own but borrowed haphazardly from both liberalism and socialism. John Paul II's insistence that Catholicism has its own sources and content of social doctrine suggests he is aware of the design to misappropriate Catholic thought as an opening to the left.

The Catholic middle emphasized a theory of limited state, private property within the common good, and a legitimate place for voluntary institutions. Aquinas was the main guide. If the state were too weak or property too concentrated, these conditions would work against the best interests of the population. Likewise, if the state were too strong and property denied the individual, this would threaten the freedom of both the people and the Church.

Philosophically, personalism came to be the theoretical basis of Catholic thought. Pius XII had already held the human person to be the origin, center, and end of all Catholic theory. The theoretical reason for this was well described by J. M. Bochenski in a book written in 1972:

> The individual man, and he alone, remains the final earthly goal of all social action, of all politics. This goal, however, can only be reached by recognizing the reality of society and its own goals. But this goal is founded in the individual welfare. The duties which we have toward society are real duties; they bind us with the same moral force as those toward individuals, for society is no fiction. Yet it remains an instrument for the fulfillment of the individual's fate.
>
> In my opinion, individualism is today no longer an important doctrine. The great debate behind the conflict of the parties and, unfortunately, the thunder of bombs, the essential debate concerning man's place in society, is taking place between the doctrines of Aristotle and Hegel. It has seldom been so clear in history as it is today what a terrible, formative, and destructive force the great philosophies can be.[25]

Bochenski's suspicion that the real struggle lies between the followers of socialism and the identification of Christianity with the followers of Hegel, against the Aristotelian tradition, seems true.

## Vocational Groups and Christian Marxism

The effort to find a concrete economic and political third way between liberalism and socialism was especially pressing for Catholics caught in countries wherein the socialists and secular liberals were philosophically doctrinaire. Here there arose, as a countermove almost in self-defense, Catholic political parties, labor unions, and employers' associations, institutions that are excoriated by the Christian left today. (The United States was in a sense unique, since neither its parties nor its unions were philosophical expressions of a world-view hostile to religion.)

At first glance, too, the logical way to proceed seemed to be the way of the nineteenth-century Christian socialists, especially the small English variety, with considerable influence from Henri de Saint-Simon's "New Christianity" and its engineering theory of how to alleviate poverty.[26] But the dogmatic theories of continental socialism, with which Rome was most familiar, propelled the Church, especially after the Russian revolution, to distinguish socialism from Communism, as Pius XI's encyclical *Divini Redemptoris* (1937) illustrates. There has been a persistent effort on the part of the Catholic left to ease Catholic social doctrine away from its Aristotelian roots toward socialism as the only valid Christian political structure, despite the deplorable record of existing socialist systems in both personal freedom and real development.

The latest attempt to make Christian thought, especially American thought, appear to be inevitably "progressing" toward a formal baptism of Marxist socialism is that of Father Arthur McGovern, S.J., in *Marxism: An American Christian Perspective*. Dale Vree, not unsympathetic to parts of the project, wrote perceptively:

> Curiously, McGovern wants to argue that it is not "logical" for atheism and materialism to be regarded as necessary components of Marxism. I disagree. This is not the place to debate the matter . . . but philosophies wedded to ambitious political movements are not always "logical."
>
> Thanks to Soviet power, Alexander Dubcek's "Socialism with a Human Face" went into early retirement—and nearby Afghanistan is a Soviet satrapy, as are far away Indochina and Cuba. More than ever, it appears that Marxism will be defined by Soviet power, not by the "logic" of a few philosophers sampling the "varieties of Marxism." One may certainly hope that normative Marxism will change—for example that it will discard its atheism and materialism—but I, for one, wouldn't waste any time waiting for that day.[27]

This underscores one of the most remarkable aspects of the whole Christian-Marxist movement, what I call the forgetfulness of Augustinian realism—the weakness of practical judgment against actual historical experience, the curious tendency of ostensibly pious Christians to allow the real Marxists to take power with religious blessings.

Another effort at a Catholic third way was corporatism, which appeared in the United States under the name Industry Council Plan or sometimes Vocational Groups. The essence of the movement was to overcome the labor-capital opposition of the Industrial Revolution by a cooperative organization embracing both, rather than in some class conflict in which one or the other had to dominate. As early as 1919, in the famous Pastoral Letter of the American Hierarchy signed by James Cardinal Gibbons (who was largely responsible for Leo XIII's permitting non-confessional labor unions on the American model in *Rerum Novarum*), we read:

> Such associations are especially needed at the present time. While the labor union or the trade union has been, and still is, necessary in the struggle of the worker for fair wages and fair conditions of employment, we have to recognize that its history, methods, and objects have made it essentially a militant organization. The time seems now to have arrived when it should be, not supplanted, but supplemented by associations or conferences composed jointly by employers and employes, which will place emphasis upon the common interests rather than the divergent aims of the two parties, upon cooperation rather than conflict.[28]

Behind this, of course, is an attempt to reject institutionally the socialist thesis of the necessity of class conflict as the natural condition of man in the industrial sector. Later some Catholic theories simply accepted class struggle and tried to give it a Christian interpretation.[29]

Still other Catholic theorists attempted to revive the idea of the medieval guild since it combined work, direction, religion, standards, and the public good in a viable institutional framework. The thought was expressed by Leo XIII and found a home for a time with the guild socialists, to reappear as distributism or the "small is beautiful" principle.

In retrospect, however, what is of most interest in the above passage from the 1919 Pastoral Letter is not only the search for a form of society that would institutionalize cooperation—the Church encouraged but never embraced the so-called cooperative movements as such—but also the irony that when a corporative form did appear in Italy and Portugal, and to some extent in the National Recovery Administration of America's New Deal, it almost proved a disaster for Catholic social doctrine. The writers of the Pastoral Letter tried valiantly to insist that the Catholic view was based on a voluntary approach, on personal and institutional freedom, rather than on the fascist corporative solution, which was in reality a form of national socialism.

The idea of vocational groups as a Catholic third way in society retained some force for a while but then was dropped. Another version of the position is that of Heinrich Pesch, S.J., probably one of the most original Catholic economists. Pesch's "solidarism" was intended as a theory of the national economy that would be neither capitalist nor socialist.[30]

Although the idea of some Christian third way is not wholly dead, thus far the experience of a union of labor and management under the direction of the state has produced something very different from what *Quadragesimo Anno* had in mind (#44).

Pius XII was interested in a version of this theory that would enable workers to become owners, retaining the theoretical basis of private property. Germany and Switzerland have been experimenting with a theory of co-management in which workers sit on management boards. Pius XII saw this as perhaps advisable but not without corresponding property rights.

Catholic thought still does not have an adequate theory of the legitimacy and autonomy of management as it has developed in recent years, though Michael Novak has been endeavoring to supply one.[31] The growing interest in ethics in management is related to the subject, but so long as there is no valid theological understanding of the nature of the modern corporation, theories of corporate ethics are likely to be closer to ideological analyses.

The corporation is probably the form by which we are most likely to be able to meet the needs and desires of the poor, particularly in view of the failure of liberal and socialist bureaucratic practices. But the famous principle of subsidiarity, the main heritage of *Quadragesimo Anno*, should be kept in mind—the idea that authority, management, and order should exist at the lowest levels possible to ensure human-sized institutions and efficiency.[32]

Two Catholic efforts to confront the effects of industrialization are related to vocational groups and have reappeared in recent years. Back in 1912 Hilaire Belloc, in *The Servile State* (a book recently reissued), warned of the growth of the state and its bureaucracy and the possibility that eventually it would take over complete care of the human being.[33] Belloc, G. K. Chesterton, and Eric Gill developed a theory of distributism, which, considered romantic at the time, has gained considerable recent attention because of E. F. Schumacher's famous *Small Is Beautiful*, a revival of Pius XI's subsidiarity principle (wryly, Schumacher called his system "Buddhist Economics," because he knew no one would take him seriously if he called it "Christian Economics").[34] The value of the distributist outlook was not apparent until after World War II, when many new nations, often poor, began to come into existence and concern developed over industrial overgrowth and pollution.

The early distributists argued for much smaller industrial units based on craft, personalism, home, and property. Until recently this was considered impractical, especially by Catholics trying to conform to modern institutions. However, the latest intellectual fad is "distributive" justice, and we can now speak of human-sized productive units.

A form of Catholic social conception that ought to be at the very center of Catholic thinking today is neither specifically distributist nor corporatist, though it is not opposed to the valuable insights of these two theories. It concentrates rather on the changes in capitalism itself. Unfortunately, the Church has never undertaken a religious, intellectual understanding of contemporary capitalism (*Laborem Exercens*, the latest social encyclical, still speaks of capitalism largely in its nineteenth-century and classical formulation) and particularly its capacity to aid the poor. Capitalism has largely been treated in a negative sense in papal documents, as an abuse of the economic system.

We need to apply to capitalism the principle that John XXIII suggested about all ideologies, that their historic practice is different from their pure formulation. Writers like Father Bernard Dempsey, S.J., Father Oswald von Nell-Breuning, Professor

Goetz Briefs, and Jacques Maritain have made significant efforts to analyze the actual form of capitalism as it has historically evolved. It is clear, despite socialist contentions, that there is a vast, almost revolutionary difference between the uncontrolled capitalism that Marx flayed and the early encyclicals confronted, and capitalism as it exists today, even in the Third World.

Until recently there has been surprisingly little effort on the part of Catholics and other Christians to analyze the forces of production and distribution in the modern economy. The rhetoric of moral righteousness has been largely cast in socialist terms, even when laced with Christian wording. There has been a strange lack of realism in the whole area.

But recent books by George Gilder, Michael Novak, Wilfred Beckermann, P. T. Bauer, and others delve into the essence of capitalism. Gilder and Novak seek in particular a theological basis for wealth production and distribution within the democratic capitalist system and a logical basis in the Judeo-Christian ethic.

Contemporary conservatism is both intellectually and politically stronger than at any previous time in the modern era. This strength is probably due to the meticulous detailing of what happens when liberal and socialist theories are put into practice. The essential element of any conservative position is its insistence on distinguishing between practice and theory, the lesson Burke learned from the French Revolution.

The intellectual exhaustion of contemporary secular liberalism and socialism has also, however, opened the way to revolutionary positions. For it is no longer believed, even by Western Marxists, that the Marxism of Russia or Eastern Europe or China is viable without naked power. For Christians to continue to opt for socialism as the answer to poverty appears to be a deliberate denial of experience.

## The Social Thought of John Paul II

Is John Paul right, left, or center? He is said to be "right" in doctrine and "left" on social matters, except for abortion. He is perhaps a minority of one—or rather, a majority of one, for he outweighs all the bishops and intellectuals in brilliance and in sanity. He is, I suspect, close to the middle, which, as Aristotle said, lies at the extreme between two wrong extremes. He will not tolerate any confusion of religion with politics. But he does not hesitate to condemn the lack of religious freedom and the violation of human rights wherever they occur. He understands the Marxist reality better than any Western religious intellectual—perhaps, indeed, better than the Marxists themselves.

With equal vigor John Paul II condemns consumerism, self-indulgence, unconcern for the poor, bias, and moral chaos. He does not see the world as divided between a wholly wrong East or Marxism and a wholly right West or capitalism. He argues for a centrality of personal and religious values that opposes both to-talitarianism and moral laxity.

The Pope seems at times overly influenced by the ecological bias that values the earth too much, at the expense of methods of helping people in need. And he does not seem to understand fully why democratic capitalism works and socialism does not.

He is extraordinarily courageous. He talks of the value of human life before the chief justice of the United States, of human rights before President Marcos, of religious freedom before his fellow Polish leaders, of religious culture before UNESCO in Paris. He tells priests to get out of politics while telling politicians they ought to aid the poor and ban weapons. He goes to Auschwitz and Hiroshima. He talks to college students and tells them to pray. He is a hero and a philosopher, a kindly man and the Pope of Rome.

Whenever I worry too much about the naïve Marxism in Catholicism today—and it is a major problem—I console myself that we have a Pope who lived under the system and survived it religiously and intellectually, something no theoretical Western Christian Marxist has done. All the varieties of political Catholicism are religiously valid only if they follow the doctrine and discipline for which the Pope stands, that faith rooted in the primacy of transcendence over politics.

# Legislating Morality: The Role of Religion

## DAVID LITTLE

THE RELATION OF GOD AND CAESAR, hardly a new problem for Christians, has been raised with fresh force by groups like Jerry Falwell's Moral Majority. These groups on the "new right" constitute a profound challenge to some established ways of thinking about religion and politics. We need to identify exactly where that challenge lies.

Falwell's position—to take him as a representative example—has a certain plausibility about it. He does not advocate establishing religion in the sense of legally requiring specific religious beliefs and worship practices.[1] He espouses free exercise of religion in keeping with what he takes to be our constitutional tradition.

On the other hand, he does advocate the legal establishment of basic public morality. The law of the land enforces standards in the essentials of a country's common life—upon such matters as the relations between the sexes, the status of women, the status of the unborn, the rearing and education of children, and the circumstances of free expression. Falwell's complaint, a complaint that consumes the new-right groups and fuels the "politics of resentment," is that the prevailing law reflects and enforces the *wrong kind* of public moral standards.

The key to Falwell's solution for the alleged degeneracy of

*David Little is professor of religion and sociology at the University of Virginia. He has a Th.D. in Christian ethics from Harvard University. Among his books is "American Foreign Policy and Moral Rhetoric: The Example of Vietnam."*

present-day America is in the name of his organization: The Moral
Majority. Since we live in a democracy, and since in democracies
majorities properly decide the legally established standards of
morality, Falwell and his associates intend to get out the vote and
change the laws. What could be more democratic than that, or
more in keeping with our inherited way of doing things? When Pat
Robertson, formerly a close associate of Falwell, says, "We have
enough votes to run the country, and when the people say, 'We've
had enough,' we're going to take over," he is striking a resonant
chord.

Two of Falwell's basic points, then, are that (1) public morality is
inevitably regulated by law, and (2) these laws ought to reflect the
beliefs of the majority of the population through "direct democracy." Another of his points is that (3) the standards he hopes to
legislate by majority rule are scriptural, or, as he puts it, "Bible-
based." He has said more than once, "We are going to single out
people in government who are against what we consider to be the
Bible, moralist position, and we're going to inform the public."

The standards Falwell advocates include the following, as expressed in his 1980 book *Listen America!:* "In spite of the fact that
the Bible clearly designates this sin [homosexuality] as an act of a
'reprobate mind' for which God 'gave them up' (Romans 1:26-28),
our government seems determined to legalize homosexuals as a
legitimate minority."[2] "Our judicial system judges human sexuality by a man-determined code of sexual conduct, not by the Word
of God."[3] Christians ought to "evaluate the stand of candidates on
moral issues" according to a "code of minimum moral standards
dictated by the Bible." These Bible-based standards yield the
following sorts of leading questions to be put to a legislator:
"Would you favor stricter laws relating to the sale of pornography?" "Do you favor laws that would increase homosexual
rights?" "Would you vote to prevent known homosexuals to teach
in schools?"[4] Finally, Falwell and others have mounted a campaign
to permit the teaching of "creationism" in the public schools, and
to legalize tax-reimbursement arrangements for parents who send
their children to Christian schools.

I mentioned that Falwell's position has a certain ring of democratic plausibility about it. If, in a democracy, one can gather majority support for particular positions on such matters as homosexuality, the status of women, and pornography, then shouldn't the law reflect these widely supported positions?

## 'The Enforcement of Morals'

Something very close to this position has been advocated by abler minds than Falwell's. Up to a point, it is the position taken by the distinguished British jurist Lord Devlin in his well-known lectures *The Enforcement of Morals*.[5] Lord Devlin says the function of the law is to preserve public order and decency and to protect citizens from what is offensive, injurious, exploitative, and corrupting. And how shall a society decide what preserves public order and decency and protects against exploitation and corruption? If, says Lord Devlin, the "vast bulk" of the community is agreed on an answer, even though a minority resolutely disagrees, a legislator is required to act on the basis of the consensus. He must do that for two reasons, summarized by Ronald Dworkin in a lucid article on the subject[6]:

> (a) In the last analysis the decision must rest on some article of moral faith, and in a democracy this sort of issue, above all others, must be settled in accordance with democratic principles.
> (b) It is, after all, the community which acts when the threats and sanctions of the criminal law are brought to bear. The community must take the moral responsibility, and it must therefore act on its own lights—that is, on the moral faith of its members.[7]

Lord Devlin would agree, then, with the first two of Falwell's positions: public morality must be legislated, and it ought to be legislated by consensus or majority rule. However, he would part company with Falwell on his third basic point, that a standard of public morality is right only if it is dictated by the Bible. Lord Devlin espouses no independent criterion of moral rightness apart from consensus. Still, if on a given question of public morality (say, homosexuality) the Falwell position is indeed the position of a "moral majority," then Lord Devlin would consider that view determinative of public morality.

Falwell and other new-right activists contend that clergy and church people have every right to participate in a political campaign aimed at changing the standards of public morality. They believe they are doing nothing different from what was done by clergymen like Martin Luther King, Jr., Ralph Abernathy, and other members of the Southern Christian Leadership Conference in the civil-rights struggle and the war on poverty in the early 1960s, or what was done by William Sloane Coffin, Jr., and other members of Clergy and Laity Concerned in the anti-war movement of the latter 1960s and early 70s. These persons supported bills and candidates that held promise of enacting their moral concerns. They used their churches as rallying points and sometimes as places of sanctuary for people who were trying to overcome racial discrimination and poverty or to redirect foreign policy. They influenced churches to take stands against "immoral laws and policies." What right, then, have these religious activists to complain now when clergy and laypeople in The Moral Majority do similar things?

Having tried to put a coherent and plausible face on the ideas of the new Christian right, I want now to argue that these ideas nevertheless represent a serious threat to the fundamental principles of a religiously pluralistic civil society like ours, and to the proper role of Christians in such a society. Americans of many different persuasions are right to be apprehensive about "the thunder on the right."

Although Falwell and company appear to be correct about the first basic feature of their position, they are seriously mistaken about the second and third features. That is, while public morality will undoubtedly have to be legislated one way or another, our pluralistic tradition rejects Falwell's and Lord Devlin's belief that public morality ought to be legislated by mere consensus, and it certainly rejects Falwell's conviction that the standards of civic morality must be "Bible-based."

In bearing the name "Baptist," Jerry Falwell is in a way a spiritual descendant of Roger Williams.[8] But Williams, the father of American religious pluralism,[9] had a profoundly different view of public morality.

To begin with, Williams drove a very large wedge between church and state:

> Now there being two states, the civil or corporeal and the ecclesiastical or spiritual, there are consequently two sorts of laws, two sorts of transgressions, two sorts of punishments, to wit, civil and spiritual, and there must be of necessity be two sorts of false or corrupt punishments, which are not just punishments . . . to wit, civil persecution and spiritual. . . .[10]

The "spiritual sword" and the "sword of steel" are two different things and ought never to be confused. That they had been manifestly confused in the Massachusetts Bay Colony (from which Williams was summarily expelled) accounted, Williams believed, for the tyranny of that community and others like it. The belief that religious conviction and practice may be subjected to coercion is itself "the bloody tenet" that disrupts both church and state.

### Roger Williams on Toleration

From this version of separationism, Williams derived a radical doctrine of religious pluralism and toleration that he extended to all forms of belief and unbelief. The right sort of political authorities will "provide in their high wisdom for the security of all the respective meetings, assemblings, worshippings, preachings, disputings, etc. . . . [so] that civil peace and the beauty of civility and humanity [may] be maintained among the chief opposers and dissenters."[11]

But Williams's grounds for favoring toleration were not only practical. It was not simply that pluralism kept the peace better than an established system, though that was important. Williams also favored toleration because he believed intensely that free, voluntary religious expression was a necessary condition of religious conviction. By no means did he favor toleration out of an indifference to religion, as Thomas Jefferson and others did.

But Williams's doctrine is still more radical than this, and he had still another reason for separating church and state as sharply as he did. Drawing upon a common Puritan emphasis, he distinguishes sharply between the first and second tables of the Decalogue, between special revelation and the duties and practices pertinent to that, on the one hand, and what he calls "the law of nature, the law moral and civil," on the other.[12] He repeatedly defends the idea that the moral and civil law is natural to every human being and provides a sufficient foundation for organizing and directing civil society. Having Christians in office is decidedly *not* required for preserving the safety and welfare of the social order. In defending the rights of non-Christians to hold political office, Williams states:

> There is a moral virtue, a moral fidelity, ability, and honesty, which other men (beside Church-members) are, by good nature and education, by good laws and good examples nourished and trained up in, that civil places need not be monopolized into the hands of Church-members (who sometimes are not fitted for them), and all others deprived of their natural and civil rights and liberties.[13]

And he goes on:

> Now what kind of magistrate soever the people shall agree to set up, whether he receive Christianity before he be set in office, or whether he receive Christianity after, he receives no more power of magistracy than a magistrate that hath received no Christianity. For neither of them both can receive more than the Commonweal, the Body of People and civil state, as men, communicate unto them, and betrust with them. . . . And hence it is true, that a Christian captain, Christian merchant, physician . . . and . . . magistrate is no more a captain . . . [or] magistrate [etc.] than a captain . . . [or] magistrate [etc.] of any other conscience or religion.[14]

Along with other liberal Puritans of the period, Williams had in the back of his mind an innovative interpretation of St. Paul's classic discussion of the state in the thirteenth chapter of the Letter to the Romans. St. Paul's admonition to obey "governing authorities" did not prescribe abject submission to any existing government. Williams and his Puritan brethren understood these words in a different way.

St. Paul asserted that "rulers are not a terror to good conduct but to bad" and that a ruler "is God's servant for your good" (literally, "God's servant to you for the sake of good"). From this Williams concluded that there existed an independent standard of public morality according to which governments might properly be judged. That is, governments are authorized by God, as Williams puts it, "for the preservation of mankind in civil order and peace (the world otherwise would be like the sea, wherein men, like fishes, would hunt and devour each other, and the greater devour the less). . . ."[15] If given regimes did not live up to the standards of good government—as Puritans like Williams believed Charles I in England did not—then such regimes forfeited their legitimacy.

Williams made much of the fact that the Roman government under which St. Paul wrote his letter to the Roman Christians was not a Christian government, nor did it, according to St. Paul's account, concern itself with enforcing the first table of the Decalogue. The only reference is to the second table—to "the commandments, 'You shall not commit adultery, you shall not kill, you shall not steal, you shall not covet . . .' "—all of which St. Paul sums up in the commandment of neighbor love (Romans 13:9, 10).

For Williams, the second table of the Decalogue, together with the second love commandment, is precisely "the law of nature, the law moral and civil," which is inscribed on the hearts of all human beings. It is the same law to which St. Paul refers earlier in the letter to the Romans when he mentions that the Gentiles, "who have not the law do by nature what the law requires" (Romans 2:14). It is this law that Williams, along with his fellow Puritans, identifies with the universal law of reason and conscience. It constitutes the basic standard of public morality according to which all legitimate magistrates are bound to rule.

When John Cotton, the ardent and eloquent defender of the establishment of religion in the Massachusetts Bay Colony, contended that "no good Christian, much less a good magistrate, can be ignorant of the Principles of saving truth," Williams fired back: "This assertion, confounding the nature of civil and moral goodness with religious, is as far from goodness, as darkness is from light."[16] In short, Williams's doctrine of the separation of church and state presupposes an important distinction between religious and moral truth. He clearly advocates a *secular* state whose peace and order can be maintained only by reference to an autonomous law of nature or reason. Moreover, this law must be observed for the health of both religion and civil society.[17]

Williams, like many of his fellow Puritans, and like John Locke, whose views are partly derivative from radical Puritan ideas, was excessively confident of the capacity of the enlightened magistrate to infer particular standards of public morality. For Williams, as for Locke, the matter of what was and what was not against public safety and welfare was evident to natural reason. Civil government should not only prohibit human sacrifice (though it is practiced for conscience' sake in places like Mexico and Peru) and prohibit prostitution (though it is sometimes performed for religious reasons) but should also impose censorship, as did "the Emperor of Rome, who censured that famous Ovid, for that wanton Book of his *De Arte amandi,* as a spark to immodesty and uncleanness. . . ." "And doubtless," Williams continues, "it is the duty of the civil sword, to cut off the incivilities of our times, as the monstrous hair of women upon the heads of some men,"[18] a prerogative to be exercised even against Quaker men who wore their tresses for conscience' sake.[19]

This self-assurance is related to Williams's confidence that there is a clean, tidy distinction between religion and civil morality. Moreover, this assurance no doubt explains Williams's apparent indifference to the task of working out a fuller theory of justice in the civil society, a theory that would take in questions of punishment and correction, economic distribution, and the relation of property-holding to political privilege. These questions were of burning significance for other Puritans during the latter 1640s.

Nevertheless, though his position is obviously incomplete, Williams makes an indispensable point about legislating public morality: *a commitment to religious pluralism must rest upon a shared belief that civil or public morality is determinable independent of religious beliefs.* Although the task of determination is not so easy as Williams believed, the principle is essential.

The most obvious implication of this is that the third basic feature of Jerry Falwell's position is mistaken. In a pluralistic society—undergirded, as I believe it is, by Williams's general assumptions—it is simply not appropriate in the public forum to give as a reason for a law or policy the fact that it is derived from the "Word of God" or is "dictated by the Bible."

## An Argument From Fairness

On closer inspection, new-right Christians like Falwell do not rely very often on purely religiously based arguments when they advocate a change in law or public policy. Take for example the familiar arguments for teaching creationism in the public schools. Creationists do not normally contend that their views on the origin of the universe ought to be taught in public schools because these views are authorized by the Bible. Rather they appeal to an "equal time" argument, which is simply an argument from ordinary fairness: in an open society, no one controversial theory ought to be "established" over others.

Interestingly enough, once this argument from fairness is introduced, it has some unanticipated and rather disturbing implications for the creationists. Once one group's theory is given equal time with the prevailing teaching in the public schools, how can other competing theories that are conscientiously held be excluded? And why not open things up beyond theories about the origin of the universe and the development of the species to include in school curricula competing theories on a whole range of other scientific and historical subjects?

Creationists frequently resort to another sort of quite secular argument, that their position is good science. They often contend that human evolution is "only a theory," which apparently means to them that it is scientifically unproved. However persuasive or unpersuasive their case may finally be, they are, in pursuing this line, no longer appealing to the authority of the Word of God. They are appealing to scientific evidence, and they must take the consequences of trying to play in that ball park!

A similar analysis could be made of the arguments of Moral Majority and like groups for a tuition-reimbursement plan. Their arguments have to do with justice (they say parents of private-school students must "pay twice" for education), equal time, free exercise of religion, and the like—not with the claim that Christian

schools ought to be supported by tuition reimbursement *simply
because* they teach God's true Word. An appeal to God's Word
does not seem to cut any ice in the political arena—nor should it.

When Falwell attacks the U.S. judicial system because it "judges
human sexuality by a man-determined code of sexual conduct, not
by the Word of God," he is again invoking an inappropriate
standard of judgment. And he repeats his mistake when he com-
plains: "In spite of the fact that the Bible clearly designates this sin
[homosexuality] as an act of a 'reprobate mind' for which God
'gave them up' . . . our government seems determined to legalize
homosexuals as a legitimate 'minority.' " The same holds for his
"Bible-based standards" that are to be used as a check-list for
appraising legislators and legislation.

In a pluralistic society, this kind of direct appeal to religious
belief as a warrant for judicial and legislative decisions constitutes
highhandedness toward other religious communities within the
society. To determine a law concerning homosexuality strictly on
the basis of the interpretations of the sacred scripture of *one*
religious tradition is about as direct an assault on the principles of
Roger Williams as one can imagine. Indeed, it has the earmarks of
"the bloody tenet." As Williams saw so clearly, once one group has
begun the process, there is nothing to stop other religious groups
from making similarly preemptory counterclaims. And since there
is no conceivable solution short of unanimous conversion to one of
the positions, the inevitable result is strife or persecution or both.

This third feature of Falwell's position, the attempt to ground
legislative proposals in parochial religious interpretations, is very
prominent in new-right thinking, and it is important that we identify it as a profound threat to our pluralistic tradition.

## Morality by Consensus

Let us return to the second and most plausible part of the Falwell
position—the view that public morality ought to be legislated by
consensus or majority rule. As we have seen, this feature can
logically be detached from the third. Lord Devlin rejected the third
feature, and yet he strongly adheres to the consensus view of public

morality, the "we-have-enough-votes-to-run-the-country" view.

Professor Ronald Dworkin's able critique of Lord Devlin's position is directly applicable to Jerry Falwell's also, and it is richly compatible with the tradition of Roger Williams that I have been attempting to shore up. Dworkin's basic criticism is neatly summarized in the following statement: "A conscientious legislator who is told a moral consensus exists must test the credentials of that consensus."[20] In other words, in matters of public morality, it is not enough to be told that the "vast bulk" of citizens holds such and such a view. Would the advocates of this mean that *any* broadly held conviction ought to be enforced as public morality? Even Lord Devlin himself, in reflecting on his earlier lectures, admitted that he might have placed "too much emphasis on feeling and too little on reason." He urges that a legislator "is entitled to disregard 'irrational' beliefs," such as the conviction—however widespread—that homosexuality causes earthquakes.[21]

This is all the opening Dworkin needs to begin to impose qualifications on the consensus theory of public morality. If the conscientious legislator may disregard *irrational* beliefs, however broad the consensus supporting them may be, Lord Devlin has already admitted *an independent standard of rationality or reasonableness* according to which we would expect a legislator to *evaluate* various proposals for legislated morality. It is not, after all, simply a matter of counting noses.

Dworkin hints, and I outwardly admit, that the chances for working out in detail a set of airtight, "objective," and universally acceptable criteria of rationality are not good. We shall have to be much more modest in this regard than Williams seems to have been. But at least we have a beachhead. There are surely some minimum standards of rationality that we must hold out for against the pure consensus theorists. Considerations like coherence and consistency of argument and respect for the rules of relevance and evidence are binding upon any legislator.

We must expect our legislators to *test* a consensus, especially when they are dealing with heated topics like homosexuality, the status of women, censorship, racial discrimination, and war and peace. Particularly at those times we shall want our legislators to ask not just *what* the people believe and want but also *why* they believe and want it.

Jerry Falwell opposes a bill that would guarantee employment rights for homosexuals. Apart from direct appeals to Scripture, which according to our earlier argument ought to be disregarded in public debate, he provides one or two other claims against treating homosexuals as "normal." "A person," he writes, "is not born with preference to the same sex, but he is introduced to the homosexual experience and cultivates a homosexual urge. It is innocent children and many young people who are victimized and who become addicts to sexual perversion."[22] This is not an argument but a mere assertion concerning a subject that is highly controversial and over which the experts rage. In the absence of evidence, Falwell's statement cannot qualify as a "reason" for anything. A conscientious legislator who was urged to vote a particular way on the basis of reasoning like this would be bound to ignore it.

Falwell writes: "If homosexuality is deemed normal, how long will it be before rape, adultery, alcoholism, drug addiction, and incest are labeled as normal?"[23] But this implied argument begs the question and assumes what it must prove. *If* homosexuality is in a class with rape, adultery, and incest, then to call one of them normal implies that the rest are normal also. But should we consider homosexuality to be in a class with rape and incest, and if so, why? Falwell provides no answer to that question. Until he does, his discussion of homosexuality ought to weigh not at all with our conscientious legislator.

My point is that if all the "reasons" for a consensus around a particular legislative proposal amount to nothing more than *assertions* like Falwell's, then the fact that the consensus is widespread is an insufficient reason for converting it into law. Perhaps plausible, even telling reasons *could* be presented. But if they haven't been, then so much the worse for the consensus.

It appears, therefore, that we cannot be satisfied with an unqualified version of the consensus or majoritarian theory of public morality. This conclusion squares with Williams's belief that an independent law of reason precedes and stands in judgment upon any given civil arrangement—an assumption that holds considerable force even if we cannot share Williams's confidence in the ready self-evidence of this law.

Yet though we must qualify the consensus theory, we cannot discard it altogether. In certain respects, societies do appear to derive their standards of public morality from prevailing assumptions. Some disputed subjects, such as abortion, sexual propriety, marital patterns, and definitions of basic health and welfare, can be resolved only by reference to the consensus of the community.[24]

But this resolution cannot be regarded as fixed and final. The history of the standards of public morality in this country and elsewhere reveals a ceaseless process of reconsideration and revision, as prevailing assumptions are challenged and debated. Public morality develops through the ongoing interaction between consensus and critical examination. This critical or rational testing of consensus has not been sufficiently considered in current popular discussions.

If a given consensus happens to include explicitly religious warrants, as do some assertions about abortion and various sexual practices, have we then discovered a point at which religious appeals are appropriate in the public arena? No. The consensus prevails not because it rests upon religious conviction but because it is a consensus. If there is no other way to resolve a question such as when life begins than by referring to some sort of nonempirical convictions, then it is rational for members of a society to give consensus its due. But the process of interaction between consensus and criticism must continue.

## A New Kind of Religious Activist?

What shall we say about the claim that the new-right religious activists are different only in message from the "old-left" activists of the 1960s and early 1970s? I have not been able to examine with care the sorts of appeal and argument made by religious leaders in the earlier period in support of political candidates and specific civil rights or anti-war legislation. My impression (and little more) is that in general the appeals are not so self-consciously or parochially religious as are the positions of the new-right Christians.

For instance, Martin Luther King made explicit and repeated appeals to the natural-law tradition, the American Constitution, and the American heritage, which were combined with rather general references to the Christian tradition and to figures like Jesus and Gandhi. He did not advocate particular "Bible-based" legislation or threaten to defeat candidates who did not conform to an explicitly religious position. And the appeals of anti-war clergy and laypeople were not so much to parochial religious warrants as to the just-war doctrine, which is a part of the natural-law tradition. Finally, I have the impression—again, very speculative—that the old-left religious activists were much more committed to public debate over the details of policies and legislation than are the new-right groups.

If these observations are accurate, the religious activists of an earlier generation exhibited a deeper commitment to a standard of public morality and to canons of public evaluation independent of religious belief than do the new-right groups. If so, they stood closer to the tradition of Roger Williams.

As often happens, Perry Miller says it best:

> For the subsequent history of what became the United States, Roger Williams possesses on indubitable importance, that he stands at the beginning of it. Just as some great experience in the youth of a person is ever afterward a determinant of his personality, so the American character has inevitably been molded by the fact that in the first years of colonization there arose this prophet of religious liberty.[25]

What is most remarkable about this early prophet of religious liberty is that he favored liberty and toleration as the fruit of his own intense religious devotion. Here was a Christian who, in the name of spreading the faith of the church, sought to limit the church's control; who, in the name of expressing his own religious convictions, accorded others the equivalent privilege; and who, in the name of practicing his religion in a community of diverse belief, submitted and committed himself to a standard of reason independent of religious belief.

His early prospects were not bright. But it was he and not his securer detractors in Massachusetts Bay who gradually captured the imagination of American religious communities, as John Courtney Murray makes powerfully clear in *We Hold These Truths*.[26] Williams's views should now be brought to the attention of the new Christian right.

The outlines of Williams's thought concerning separation of church and state, toleration, and the civil order and public morality also suggest some lessons for other religious groups. The principal one, in my view, is the need to cultivate a "divided consciousness." That means assuming a difference between the "two cities," and remembering that the terms of discourse and relationship in the two are not interchangeable. The history of religious life in this country, starting with Massachusetts Bay, has frequently been marred by the neglect of that distinction: Jerry Falwell's proposals for "Bible-based laws" are only the most recent instance.

Unqualified religious appeals have no place in civil discourse over the legislation of public morality. What are appropriate, as Williams saw so clearly, are appeals to autonomous and common standards of reason. Therefore, if Christians are going to involve themselves in the public arena (as they have every right to do), then they must learn to play by the rules. The task of divining the proper application of the "law moral and civil" is often difficult, but it is a task we cannot refuse.

# The Moral-Religious Basis of Democratic Capitalism

## MICHAEL NOVAK

IN THIS NINETIETH YEAR after Pope Leo XIII's letter *Rerum Novarum* it is clear that the churches—the Christian churches, Catholic and Protestant—have become increasingly involved in the discussion of economic questions. The frequency of economic statements from the Vatican, the World Council of Churches, the National Council of Churches, and various other Christian bodies has been increasing.

Yet no other field within the range of view of theology has a thinner and poorer theological literature than economics. The books or chapters in which major or even minor theologians deal with economic questions occupy a very small shelf in the theological library.

Increasingly, however, economics is becoming a concern of the churches, in part because in the real world economics is becoming the predominant political concern. The leaders of nations probably spend more time on domestic and international economic issues than on any others. Like it or not, then, those involved in religion

---

*Michael Novak is a resident scholar in religion and public policy at the American Enterprise Institute in Washington, D.C. He formerly taught at Stanford and at Syracuse University, where he was the Ledden-Watson Distinguished Professor of Religion. He is the author of twelve books, including "The Rise of the Unmeltable Ethnics" and (forthcoming) "The Spirit of Capitalism." This essay is based on the transcript of an oral presentation.*

54

and theology will have to learn a great deal about economics in the coming generation. They will need to develop economic theology just as they have in recent years developed historical theology and political theology.

## A Three-Level Theology

This theology of economics will be worked out on three different levels. First, there will properly be a theology of economics dealing with the general concepts on which economic life is based—such things as scarcity, wealth, poverty, production, and distribution. A theology of economics will need to describe these very general realities of human life and attempt to determine their meaning for religion and religion's meaning for them. For instance, poverty and scarcity are present in all eras. What is the significance of, say, productivity for religion, and what is the significance of religion for productivity?

The second level will concern the particular economic systems that have been invented, of which there are remarkably few. A theology of economics will go through these systems—including feudalism, slavery, mercantilism, capitalism, and socialism—to show the meaning of each for religion and religion for it. This second level will involve first a thorough understanding of the different systems and then some comparative work.

The third level of discourse will involve us with certain particulars within systems. A prime example would be the multinational corporation. A considerable amount of work will be required to understand the multinational corporation in religious terms and to deal with its problems and alternatives to it. In an interdependent world of our sort, all economic activities will have an international dimension—and if not through multinational corporations, then how?

I have found it useful to keep these levels of discourse clearly in mind, because often arguments conducted as though they were aimed at one or another are actually on a quite different level. Here I want to concentrate on the second level, the discussion of the systems, and particularly the system of democratic capitalism. I would like to give a few indications of how I think a theology of capitalism might be developed.

Since there are only approximately 160 nations in the world, we can be rather concrete in talking about systems rather than generalizing about types. By democratic capitalism, I mean the system in the United States and those few other systems in the world that to one degree or another may be described as like ours. No two are identical; our system is not like that of the British, or the Japanese, or the West Germans. There are, perhaps, twenty or so nations that might be called democratic capitalist, analogously. It is useful to concentrate on each, case by case. Here I keep in mind the United States.

### Conservatives Against Capitalism

For almost 200 years now, there has been, especially among humanists and among social scientists, a rather pronounced bias against the *economic* component of our system. Capitalism has had many more opponents than proponents among scholars and writers. Often these opponents have often come from the conservative side. There is a substantial anti-capitalist literature written by literary conservatives of various sorts, like T. S. Eliot and Evelyn Waugh. F. R. Leavis says the main theme of British literature for 300 years has been "Luddite," and I think he might more exactly say "anti-capitalist," from the dark satanic mills that Blake described to the novels of Dickens, and in most literary commentary. The columnist George Will, who writes an anti-capitalist column about every three months, describes himself as a stained-glass conservative. I prefer to think of him as a rose-trellis conservative, by which I mean that sort of civilized literary conservative who abhors neon lights and busy streets and skyscrapers and supermarkets and competition and who really thinks that Britain was a more civilized place when there was a rose trellis over every rural cottage doorway—dirt floors and outdoor privies, but a rose trellis over the door. Surprisingly, the strength of the anti-capitalist sentiment among conservatives is very clear. It is also clear among the writers of what is called the modern Catholic Renaissance—Belloc, Eric

Gill, Lamennais, Gabriel Marcel. And so anyone who begins the quest for a theology of capitalism begins in the midst of a hundred objections to democratic capitalism, many on aesthetic or moral-religious grounds.

I would like to make four comments about moral and religious qualities in democratic capitalism. First, a system like ours is really three systems in one: a political, an economic, and a moral-cultural system. This design is based in part on a theology of sin. Each of the three systems has a certain independence of the other two. Each has its own institutions and its own leaders. Each attracts a different type of human personality, and the types don't necessarily like or trust one another. That's part of the design. It says on our coins, "In God We Trust"—meaning, in nobody else.

Many people I have known in religion or literature do not understand the symbols on the financial pages of the *New York Times* or the *Wall Street Journal*. They do not understand what makes those symbols move in one direction or another. And they lead perfectly happy lives. I know many people in business or economics who don't pay attention to what Hans Küng or other theologians are saying. They don't read the latest philosophers or literary critics. And they lead perfectly happy lives. It seems to be required that political persons know little about economics or business. And they nevertheless can lead perfectly happy lives.

The system was designed to separate church from state, university from state, press from state—to separate the moral-cultural system and its institutions from the state, the economic institutions from the state. This is what makes our sort of system so distinctive. All previous systems were unitary, so that one set of authorities would make essentially all the basic economic and political decisions, and generally most of the moral-cultural decisions as well. We have seen in Iran a kind of relapse into that sort of system. That is the classic pattern of human history, the traditional society.

The *political system* we cherish is based on rights—maybe above all the individual's right to pursue happiness, which is an extraordinary conception, an extraordinary right. Our system is one of rights and procedures, of due process, of suffrage. The *economic system* is built around a perception of the way in which a market can bring about order—a counterintuitive perception, that one. It is built around incentives, extraordinary forms of cooperation and invention, the creativity of intellect, and the institutions set up to stimulate that creativity. The third component, the *moral-cultural system*, is liberal, pluralistic. No one sacred canopy stretches over our society defining the kind of beliefs or visions that each of us must hold. Our society does not compel us to share a single vision; it deliberately keeps at its heart a kind of emptiness based on respect for what a human being is and what human societies are.

Just as the traditional unitary societies owe a great deal to traditions of monotheism, I think it is not absurd to suggest that the doctrine of the Trinity has had an important cultural effect on imagination and possibility, helping us to imagine pluralism in almost everything. Perhaps our differentiation of systems has something to do with our conception of God—whom we conceive of both as a community and as one.

## A Sense of Community

This brings me to a second moral-theological basis of this system: its sense of community. It is often supposed that democratic capitalism is uniquely given to the individual, even in a destructive way. This is the great accusation against capitalism made continually by the popes and often by theological and religious writers.

But there is another motif in the actual practice of democratic capitalism that is profound and powerful, though the philosophy of individualism that dominated Great Britain during the rise of capitalism hid it from us. Adam Smith called his book "An Inquiry into the Nature and Causes of the Wealth [not of individuals and not of Great Britain or of Scotland but] of *Nations*," and he intended the argument to apply to all humankind. He was trying to imagine a system that would raise the material base of humankind. His motive was fundamentally social and universal.

Moreover, the distinctive social invention of this system is that organized form of cooperation called the corporation. The economic task is so complex and difficult that no one person can achieve it alone, nor can any one generation achieve it alone. An institution that extends across the generations was needed. And so the corporation came into being as a voluntary and cooperative association aimed at fulfilling certain economic tasks that no one person can do alone. That, too, offers a suggestion that the system is not nearly so individualistic as we think. And it sheds some light on why we also worry about the American's being too much the conformist, the organization man, the joiner, the belonger. There's as much evidence on that side as on the side that we are anarchic individualists.

A third indication of our bent toward community is the social sense we nourish in our children. My eight-year-old daughter has more friends to visit and meetings to attend than her two parents can possible provide transportation for. She is not brought up as a lonely, isolated individual. She is brought up as a joiner, a be-longer, a cooperator, a member of associations of many sorts. These cooperative skills are essential to both our political and our economic life. In cultures where people lack skills of cooperation, organization, teamwork, and practical compromise—and in many cultures these are rare—a system like ours cannot work.

## The Right to Transform History

A third moral-religious point to be made about democratic capitalism has to do with transforming history. Judaism and Christianity imagine the religious vocation as a demand that believers try to change history—not to escape from history, but to bring about God's will on earth as it is in heaven. They foster the belief that the Lord is the Lord of history, and so it is right and obligatory to try to change history. An anthropologist in Belgium, Leo Moulin, wrote a book about economic development (*L'Aventure Européene*, 1972) in which he tried to find out who invented what and why. Why did so many of the fundamental inventions, including the mining of things from the bowels of the earth, develop in Jewish and Christian lands? For people to believe that they would not be punished by the gods for bringing things forth from this darkness and transforming them requires a certain vision of the gods and their relation to nature. Not by accident, Professor

Moulin argues, did the theory of intelligence built around invention and discovery—a theory that has enormous significance for economics—develop under the tutelage of Christianity and Judaism.

Democratic capitalism depends on a sense of development and invention and creativity, and it therefore values intelligence highly. This emphasis led to the invention of a new form of justice, the fourth and final point I want to make about the moral-religious basis of capitalism. In pre-modern literature, most treatises on justice have a great deal to say about *distributive* justice, but it had not entered into the mind of man to imagine that he had an obligation to *produce*, to create wealth. It was John Locke who first glimpsed this possibility, and Adam Smith who thought through its economic implications. Locke noted that if you took the field in all of Great Britain that was most favored by nature and then applied to it the best of agricultural science—and this, remember, was the seventeenth century—you could increase the yield of that field not twofold, not tenfold, but a hundredfold. The application of intelligence would show that the Creator made the world infinitely more wealthy than earlier ages had thought. And so slowly but steadily the idea of economic development came into being.

Adam Smith's inquiry into the wealth of nations was the pioneering book. He observed that the world did not have limits, that it was not static, and that wealth was not fixed once and for all. There are secrets hidden in the earth by the Creator. And there is a corresponding capacity hidden in human beings by the Creator to bring to light the earth's hidden wealth. Oil lay under the sands of Arabia for five thousand years. It was known about, but what was it good for? Ink, a little perfume. Then the invention of the piston conferred enormous wealth on the Arab nations. Things that today we count as valuable resources were dismissed or ignored a century or two ago. And what we dismiss and ignore today may at some future time be enormously precious. (It seems to me absolutely unfair that recent investigation shows that the silicon recoverable from sand is useful for microcomputers. One would think the Arabs had enough with the oil under the sand—will they become rich all over again from the sand itself? Nobody ever said that God was fair.)

In former times a favorite image of evil was the miser. Because wealth was considered to be fixed and finite, the miser who sat in his counting house counting up his money was subtracting money from the common store. That was a vicious act. With the invention of democratic capitalism, the miser became no longer an evil figure but a ridiculous one, for wealth could now be invested to create new wealth.

There was now a productive ethic. The world of the year 1800 had 800 million souls in it, most of whose lives were nasty, brutish, and short. Famines racked London or Paris every fifteen or twenty years, killing as many as ten thousand people; the average life expectancy in France in 1800 was twenty-seven for females, twenty-four for males. Those who could produce more food, shelter, and clothing by using intelligence were suddenly acquiring an obligation to do so. Justice now imposed an obligation upon those who could produce, that they should. Justice, then, has a productive as well as a distributive dimension, and the first is a precondition of the second.

There are other things that might be said about the moral-cultural system integral to the capitalist economy and the democratic polity. But, with due respect for limits assigned here, I must conclude with one observation. No realistic theology of the world, or of the laity, or of work, is conceivable until we have placed the theology of economics on a sounder basis. For all practical purposes, this will mainly involve a theology of democratic capitalism. For that is politically the freest and economically the most prosperous of the social systems in which Christians and Jews today find themselves.

# Ethics, Power, and U.S. Foreign Policy

## WHITTLE JOHNSTON

WHAT ROLE CAN A CHRISTIAN political ethic play in contemporary American foreign policy? To investigate this question we shall examine six areas: ethics, political ethics, and the effect of a Christian outlook upon political ethics; foreign policy generally, U.S. foreign policy, and the impact of current realities upon U.S. foreign policy.

These six areas entail problems at very different levels of generality. We should bear in in mind that controversy at one level does not necessitate controversy at all levels. Moreover, as we move from the more general to the more specific, the quality of ethical analysis we can make is closely related to the accuracy of our empirical knowledge.

According to Aristotle, ethics is the study of the good:

> Since then of all things which may be done there is some one End which we desire for its own sake, and with a view to which we desire everything else; and since we do not choose in all instances with a further end in view (for then men would go on without limit, and so the desire would be unsatisfied and fruitless), this must be the Chief Good, i.e., the best thing of all.[1]

---

*Whittle Johnston is professor of government and foreign affairs at the University of Virginia. He has a Ph.D. from Harvard University. He has lectured on international politics at the Foreign Service Institute and before many other groups, and he is completing a two-volume study on the foreign policy of Woodrow Wilson.*

Reinhold Niebuhr gives us a more specific insight into the character of the good:

> ... evil is always the assertion of some self-interest without regard to the whole, whether the whole be conceived as the immediate community, or the total community of mankind, or the total order of the world. The good is, on the other hand, always the harmony of the whole on its various levels.[2]

From Immanuel Kant we draw the third element in our conception of ethics, that it presupposes freedom:

> Hence man can regard himself from two points of view and similarly can come to know laws for the exercise of his faculties and consequently laws for all his actions. *First,* so far as he belongs to the world of sense, man is himself subject to the laws of nature (heteronomy); *second,* so far as he belongs to the intelligible world, [man is] under laws independent of nature. ... Now we see that when we conceive ourselves as free we transfer ourselves into the world of intellect and recognize the autonomy of the will with its consequence, morality. ...[3]

*Ethics,* then is the effort of free men to *understand the meaning of the good,* conceived as the harmony of the parts with the whole, and *ethical action* is the effort of free men to *achieve the good,* conceived as the harmony of self-interest with the larger social whole.

Ethical behavior is unintelligible, as Kant maintained, without the *autonomy* or freedom of the will. To the degree that man is subject to the laws of nature, his behavior cannot be understood as ethical. To the degree that a man's actions are determined, by either internal or external constraints, they cannot rightly be called ethical. Responsibility presupposes freedom. It is a perverse exercise of moral judgment to praise or condemn a person for actions whose outcomes were determined independent of his will. Similarly, a person's sense of guilt over a particular outcome is ethical only in proportion to his responsibility for that outcome. Man's ethical awareness does not confer upon him an automatic justification for feeling guilty. There is false guilt as well as false pride.

We may tentatively state as the highest standard of ethical excellence for the individual that he freely will the well-being of others as strongly and consistently as he wills his own, and as the highest standard for the community that each member freely will the good of all the others as strongly and consistently as he wills his own. A community with this standard approaches the achievement of perfect harmony between the citizen and society, and its members approach fully responsible behavior.

This standard logically implies that behavior resulting from coercion is deprived of ethical content. Jean Jacques Rousseau put vividly the contrast between force and right:

> Force is a physical power; I do not see what morality can result from it. . . . If we admit that force constitutes right, the effect changes with the cause: all force which overcomes the first succeeds to its right. As soon as men can disobey with impunity, they can do so justifiably; and because the strongest is always in the right, strength is the only thing men should seek to acquire. But what sort of right is that which perishes with the force that gave it existence? If it is necessary to obey by force, there can be no occasion to obey from duty; and when force is no more, all obligation ceases with it. We see, therefore, that this term "right" adds nothing to force, but is indeed an unmeaning term.[4]

Rousseau developed this argument to show that the phrase "the right of the strongest" was meaningless, and to defend his brilliant alternative formulation: "The strongest is never strong enough to be always the master, unless he transforms strength into right, and obedience into duty."[5]

In these passages Rousseau views the ethical problem primarily from the standpoint of those who are victims of coercion, and insists that they have no moral obligation to yield to it. If we turn his perspective upon those who seek to impose their will on others, we arrive at another formulation. The behavior of an individual or group is deprived of ethical content to the degree that the individual or group seeks its own well-being at the expense of others'. Consistent assertion of self-interest at the expense of the whole is a complete degradation of ethical standards.

The behavior of the *coerced* is deprived of ethical content to the degree it is deprived of freedom; the behavior of the *coercer* is deprived of ethical content to the degree he seeks to deprive others of their freedom. Freedom takes on a very different significance in the two contexts, as Abraham Lincoln saw clearly:

The shepherd drives the wolf from the sheep's throat, for which the sheep thanks the shepherd as a *liberator,* while the wolf denounces him for the same act as the destroyer of liberty, especially as the sheep was a black one. Plainly the sheep and the wolf are not agreed upon a definition of the word liberty. . . .[6]

Hans Morgenthau gives a different formulation of the same problem:

Political freedom, then, has two different and incompatible meanings according to whether we think of the holder or the subject of political power. Freedom for the holder of political power signifies the opportunity to exercise political domination; freedom for the subject means the absence of such domination.[7]

Freedom, as Kant maintained, is the condition of an ethical act by any individual. But political freedom, in Lincoln's view, may be the means whereby some persons seek to deprive others of the very possibility of ethical action. For Kant's insight to serve as a guide to ethical action he had to give it a more precise formulation: "So act as to treat humanity, both in your own person and in that of others, as an end in itself, and never as a means only."[8] As William Yandell Elliott has observed, Kant goes beyond Rousseau

. . . by insisting that no power could ethically deprive the individual of his own right to accept or reject the moral values which he was asked by the community to obey. That way ("forcing men to be free") lay totalitarianism—e.g., Marxism. . . . Kant drew the necessary consequences for such a universal formulation of individual moral responsibility by showing that in a true ethical community the protection of voluntary action must be maintained.[9]

The divergences among Christians on political ethics have been said to reflect "differing emphases given to the objectives of justice, freedom, and order."[10] Let us see how these objectives are related to what we have observed about the nature of ethical activity. *Freedom* is the condition of any ethical action. *Justice* is the harmony of the parts with the whole achieved through equality in freedom. Freedom and equality are the regulative principles of justice. Through the equal protection of voluntary action the claim to freedom is itself prevented from becoming an instrument of coercion. *Order* is the protection of the community against violence to life and to property. It, too, signifies a harmony of the parts with the whole at this most basic level of the community's life. While order is not a sufficient condition for the achievement of justice, it is a necessary one.

## Particular Problems of Political Ethics

Politics is an aspect of group behavior. While individuals have, at best, had a very mixed success in trying to bring their behavior into accord with ethical standards, efforts to bring group behavior into such accord have been far more difficult. In the *Federalist Papers* Alexander Hamilton highlighted one of the sources of this moral shortfall in group behavior:

> Has it been found that bodies of men act with more rectitude or greater disinterestedness than individuals? The contrary of this has been inferred by all accurate observers of the conduct of mankind; and the inference is founded upon obvious reasons. Regard to reputation has a less active influence, when the infamy of a bad action is to be divided among a number, than when it is to fall singly upon one.[11]

Niebuhr argued repeatedly that the collective conscience of groups was ordinarily far weaker than the conscience of individuals.

Another source of the relative ethical deficiency of group behavior is that groups—and states in particular—depend for their cohesion on factors that are not "ethical" at all. We have observed that the behavior of a group may be considered ethical only to the degree that each member in it freely wills the group's well-being as vigorously as he wills his own. If each member so willed, the group would enjoy perfect cohesion.

However, few groups—and no state—achieve their cohesion on so pure an ethical basis. The family itself is based in part on *natural* factors, on the sexual impulse that draws the individual outside himself. States too depend for their cohesiveness in part upon nature, often through the contribution that geographic and ethnic factors make to their unity, nearly always through the economic benefits drawn from the more extensive division of labor that takes place within them. Beyond these natural factors are *historical* ones, for the cohesion of peoples often develops through historical "accidents" that place them in a common circumstance, and give them a common memory. From these original bases of unity that are largely amoral (and occasionally immoral) there emerges a capacity for collective action through a thousand and one specific adjustments worked out over a very long time. Edmund Burke has given us the classic formulation of the relation between historical factors and group cohesion:

> Our constitution is a prescriptive constitution; it is a constitution whose sole authority is that it has existed time out of mind. . . . Prescription is the most solid of all titles, not only to property, but, which is to secure that property, to government. . . . It is a better presumption even than the *choice* of a nation, far better than any sudden and temporary arrangement by actual election. Because a nation is not an idea only of local extent, and individual momentary aggregation; but it is an idea of continuity, which extends in time as well as in numbers and space. And this is a choice not of one day, or one set of people, not in a tumultuary and giddy choice; it is a deliberate election of the ages and of generations; it is a constitution made by what is ten thousand times better than choice, it is made by the peculiar circumstances, occasions, tempers, dispositions, and moral, civil, and social habitudes of the people, which disclose themselves only in a long space of time. . . .[12]

Nationality as a basis of cohesion is sometimes seen as a fact of nature, sometimes as consciously willed, sometimes as the product of historical evolution. Burke's analysis of nationality in the above passage puts primary weight on its historic dimension. Ernest Renan, partly in reaction against historical emphases, stressed the importance of consent: "A nation is a soul, a spiritual principle. . . . It presupposes a past; but it resumes itself in the present by a tangible fact: the consent, the clearly expressed desire to continue life in common. The existence of a nation is a plebiscite of every day."[13] For others, the defining element of nationality is to be found in its ethnic content, biologically determined.

The old adage that there must be honor even among thieves suggests that the capacity for cooperative behavior is evidence of the presence of virtue in a group. We have set as one criterion of ethical achievement the degree to which the interest of the part is harmonized with the interest of the whole. Yet, knowing that group cohesion depends in part on natural and historical factors, we cannot draw any exact correlation between the cohesion of a group and the justice of its common life. Because the bases of cooperative behavior are rooted in far more than good will, it is possible to have an extensive and intensive group cohesion that is sustained only slightly by ethical factors. It is also possible to have group cohesion quite limited in extent and intensity that rests substantially on ethical factors. In evaluating the ethical aspect of group cohesion, we must pay less attention to the fact that such cohesion exists than to the way it is achieved.

There is another way in which a group's dependence on natural and historical factors for its cohesion affects the ethical judgments we can make of it. The ethical commitment—particularly in its Christian and Kantian embodiments—pushes toward the universal. The central mystery that Kant sought to resolve in his ethical theory was how man should acknowledge some obligations as universally binding. His categorical imperative is explicit in its universalism: "Act as if the maxim of your action were to become by your will a universal law of nature."[14] Yet the natural and historical factors that contribute to group cohesion fall far short of the universal. To the degree that the individual's loyalty to the group derives from these factors, it, too, falls short of the universal, and he comes to define his vested interests in terms of his group. Beyond this, the group often seeks a full claim upon the individual's conscience—seeks to harness his sense of obligation to purposes of the group.

The ethical complexities that attend all group behavior are particularly intense in state behavior. With most groups the individual can choose whether to be a member. Not so with the state. If he does have a choice, it is between membership in his given state or membership in another. The plight of those outside the state altogether—those who belong to no state at all—is among the most pathetic of all conditions in our world. Furthermore, the state considers its claim upon the individual's allegiance to have a greater legitimacy than any other group's claim.

With these considerations in mind, Hans Morgenthau stresses a twofold corruption of the state: not only does it become the repository of its citizens' drive to power, but it also transforms the nature of that drive:

> While society puts liabilities upon aspirations for individual power, it places contributions to the collective power of the state at the top of the hierarchy of values. All these factors work together to stimulate the individual's lust for power and to give its manifestations a free rein, as long as the individual seeks power not for himself directly, but for the state. . . . What here takes place is a formidable perversion of the moral sense itself, an acquiescence in evil in the name of the very standards which ought to condemn it.[15]

Ethical evaluation of state behavior, as distinguished from other forms of behavior, is further complicated by the most special of the claims made by the state, the claim to a monopoly on the legitimate use of force. If, as Rousseau argued, the right of the strongest is a meaningless concept since right and force are antithetical entities, then on what ethical grounds can the state's use of force be justified? The problem of justification involves both an internal and an external dimension, both the police power and the war power.

## Man Outside the State

The degree of force that states have felt they could legitimately claim has varied enormously in different periods, and in different circumstances within the same period. The contrast between the views of Hobbes and the views of Locke casts light on this point. For Hobbes, man in the "state of nature" (i.e., outside the state, or before the existence of the state) is devoid of any ethical sense or social bonds, totally absorbed in his egotistical preoccupations, in "a war of all against all." Only a grant of unrestricted power to the sovereign can be expected to bring about order. To be sure, there is always a risk, in the unrestricted grant of power, that the sovereign will violate the fundamental interests of the subjects. But, unless the sovereign threatens life itself, men must choose the strong state, even with its dangers to justice, over the anarchy of the state of nature, where no order is possible.

Man in Locke's state of nature is very different, for he has a moral sense and a capacity for significant social relations. He enters the state, not because order and justice are unattainable outside it, but to remedy the inconveniences of pursuing order and justice in the state of nature. There is, accordingly, no need to endow the sovereign with unlimited coercive power; a limited grant is all to which it can legitimately lay claim.

The distinction between Hobbes and Locke on this point reminds us that the legitimacy of the state's claim to force cannot be determined outside the larger social context—both internal and external—within which state activity takes place. We noted in examining social cohesion that its ethical dimension could not be assessed without detailed empirical knowledge of the role that non-moral factors played in the presence (or absence) of that cohesion. Similar considerations should govern our assessment of the legitimacy of the state's claim to use force. This depends on our estimate of the gravity of the consequences likely to follow from the state's failure to use the necessary level of force. That, in turn, cannot be determined without detailed empirical knowledge of the larger social context.

One cannot, in short, give a determinate general answer to the question of what level of force falls within ethical bounds, or the degree to which force does or does not further the achievement of ethical ends. Paul Ramsey rightly informs us that the covenant with Noah "legitimates government's use of evil to restrain greater evil."[16] Were a particular state the sole source of unwarranted coercion, it would be open to clear ethical condemnation. But the sources of coercion are multiple, both within the state and in the external world of anarchy. Ethical evaluation of a state's use of force must, accordingly, always be set against the ethical deprivations that would result from the use of force by other sources, unchecked by the force of the state in question.

Awareness that state behavior inevitably falls short of moral norms need not lead us to the position adopted by prominent spokesmen for the "realist" school (e.g., Hans Morgenthau) that politics is fundamentally different from other areas of ethics and that ethical evaluation of state actions is largely futile. Knowing that the freedom of states is always restricted, we need not infer that there is *no* freedom, or that variations in the degree of freedom present are without great ethical significance. While we realize that the authority behind government action is often diffuse and the assignment of responsibility difficult, we are not entitled to conclude that determining degrees of responsibility is impossible, or unimportant. From a recognition that all states employ force in support of their policies, we cannot infer that the circumstances and degree of its use are secondary matters. The understanding that all states draw their unity from more than ethical sources, and all fall short of achieving a just unity, does not absolve us of the responsibility of assessing the relative justice and freedom of that unity.

The primary undertaking of ethical analysis in political matters should be to determine degrees of "more or less." Emphasis on the measure to which all states' behavior falls short of ethical norms should be taken not to exhaust our responsibility but rather to concentrate it upon the obligation to clarify proximate distinctions.

The ethical elements of political activity are always intertwined with nonethical (and frequently unethical) components. An effective political ethic cannot, therefore, be confined within the framework of ethical analysis. The quality of ethical evaluation cannot be divorced from the quality of empirical analysis, for only through the latter can we begin to disentangle the specifically ethical components of the problem at hand. Empirical knowledge is the precondition for meaningful definition of the problem itself.

## How Christianity Affects Political Ethics

The Christian, beyond his obligation to the state, has also an obligation to God. Jesus instructed the Christian to "render unto Caesar the things which are Caesar's; and unto God, the things that are God's" (Matthew 22:21). The determination of what is God's due and what is Caesar's has always been a highly complex and controversial matter.

The prevailing tradition of the Middle Ages derived from the formulation by Pope Gelasius I of the doctrine of the two swords, or the two authorities. To be sure, this did not lay to rest all controversy, as the subsequent struggle of the Papalists and the Imperialists illustrated. Nor could it provide authoritative guidance when church unity was broken by the Protestant Reformation.

Despite Martin Luther's strong personal inclination toward freedom of conscience in matters of faith, the weight of his influence was to condemn resistance to state authority, as in this:

> It is in no wise proper for anyone who would be a Christian to set himself up against the government, whether it act justly or unjustly.
>
> There are no better works than to obey and serve all those who are set over us as superiors. For this reason also disobedience is a greater sin than murder, unchastity, theft, and dishonesty. . . .[17]

Although John Calvin was even more explicit than Luther in condemning resistance to constituted authority, where Calvinists found themselves in a minority (notably in Scotland under John Knox) they insisted it was the duty of Christians to correct rulers when they acted contrary to God's teaching. In Knox's words:

> For now the common song of all men is, we must obey our kings, be they good or be they bad; for God hath so commanded. But horrible shall the vengeance be, that shall be poured forth upon such blasphemers of God his holy name and ordinance. For it is no less blasphemy to say that God hath commanded kings to be obeyed when they command impiety, than to say that God by his precept is author and maintainer of all iniquity.[18]

The dual commitment of the Christian, interpreted in varying ways in differing circumstances, has been the most decisive single factor in shaping the distinctive course of Western political history. For the pagan, the emperor was both the supreme civil authority and a divinity. But the Christian owed allegiance both to his earthly ruler and to God. In the words of George Sabine:

> This double aspect of Christian society produced a unique problem which in the end contributed perhaps more than any other to the specific properties of European political thought. Far beyond the period in which the relation of the two authorities was a chief controversial issue, the belief in spiritual autonomy and the right of spiritual freedom left a residuum without which modern ideas of individual privacy and liberty would be scarcely intelligible.[19]

The Christian's determination to seek to obey God's wi. its ethical embodiment in the Golden Rule—put him in oppositio. to the exercise of political power that did violence to that will. His religious commitment had an explicit ethical content that could not leave him indifferent to how political power was exercised. He stood under the obligation to measure a particular political order against the standards of a just political order. Paul Ramsey states the central problem:

> Today, ships of state sail between this Charybdis and that Scylla, between the claims of justice and the need for order. Through this narrow defile we must seek the answer to the final question: What are the prospects for peaceful change in the direction of greater justice and security among states?[20]

The resources for resolving this problem, or at least for lessening its severity, are to be found in the rich Christian moral tradition. Christianity affirms the existence of objective ethical standards independent of the judgment of ruler or citizen and binding upon both. According to these standards, the Christian is obligated to seek to bring his will into accord with God's, that is, with the selfless love, the *agape,* of the Gospels. He is obligated also to seek the good of other men as fervently as he seeks his own. To the degree that a society shares a common faith in this Higher Law and tries to carry out its ethical implications, that society has the resources for moving toward a reconciliation between the claims of order and the claims of justice.

## The Christian View of Man

The Christian understanding of politics is derived from the Christian understanding of human nature and human history. Man's inclination toward evil is rooted in his most distinctive quality, the one that sets him apart from the world of nature—his freedom of will. This freedom makes possible his defiance of God's will, his fall from the innocence of the Garden, his original sin. Man's gift of freedom, however, may also enable him to realize that the perversion of his own special gifts is at the root of his ethical failings, and to allow God's grace to help him contain the destructive potential of his freedom and nourish its creative possibilities.

Some secular philosophies offer fragmentary equivalents of the Christian view. According to Hobbes, human nature is wholly egotistical, bound by no obligation to any law higher than self-interest; and so man in his political life is faced with a stark choice: anarchy at the price of unending war, or order at the risk of unrestrained tyranny. But in Locke's view, because man is bound by an objective moral law higher than the self, the state is a *supplement* to his capacity for moral action rather than a *substitute* for something he does not have. The role of the state is to secure the bases of order and thereby enhance the possibilities for justice. Both ruler and subject, however, are bound by a Higher Law that defines the rights and duties of both. While the citizen has an obligation to obey the law and the state has a right to enforce it, the state has an obligation to use its power justly and the citizen has a right to resist unjust uses. A tyranny, for Locke, was a state that exercised power in violation of justice and expected citizens to offer obedience in the absence of rights. Locke's conception of the role of governance and of citizenship corresponds profoundly with elements in the Christian view of man and of history.

The conviction that both ruler and subject had both rights and duties underlay Locke's view of government as a social contract between the two. The conception of a contract binding on both parties was an idea with great political and ethical significance, containing three specific insights. First, the state's claim to provide order is an insufficient ethical basis for allegiance to it. Second, the ethical problem is not a choice between order and justice but a quest for the reconciliation of order with justice. Third, this reconciliation is made possible when both parties acknowledge their obligations to a higher moral law.

Hedley Bull provides a significant contemporary clarification of the relation between justice and order by indicating the components of "order":

> First, all societies seek to ensure that life will be in some measure secure against violence resulting in death or bodily harm. Second, all societies seek to ensure that promises, once made, will be kept, or that agreements, once undertaken, will be carried

out. Third, all societies pursue the goal of ensuring that the possession of things will remain stable to some degree. . . .[21]

Bull then proceeds to weigh the priority that should be assigned to the claims of order as against the claims of justice. On the basis of the preceding analysis, I suggest that this is a misleading way of casting the issue. In the history of political thought we note a progression from Hobbes's view of "order," that it was protection through a strong state against private violence, to Locke's broader conception of order as protection against both private violence and state violence. This development would have been impossible, however, without a simultaneous growth in understanding of the conditions of political justice, i.e., of what was the right constitution of the state itself.

Similar considerations apply to the second component of Bull's view of order—the need that promises be kept. The social-contract theorists understood that the most basic of all promises was the one between a government and its citizens, and that the viability of all lesser promises was dependent on this great one.

The third element in Bull's view of order, the need to ensure some stability of possession, is in turn dependent on the effectiveness of a particular kind of promise—e.g., guarantees of title to property. We should be on guard, then, against the notion that the conditions of order can be neatly separated from the conditions of justice, or that there is some clearly defined sequential relation between the two.

The Christian understanding of man confirms the two conclusions about the problem of political ethics we drew previously. It enables us to understand how, given the limitations of human nature, all political behavior—indeed, all of human behavior—falls short of the ultimate norms. It also helps us understand that possibilities for proximate justice are open to man in his political life and to direct our ethical awareness to determining the degree of justice and order achieved.

However, the Christian orientation sets these understandings in a metaphysical framework that greatly deepens their foundation and extends their range. The limitations of ethical achievement are understood to derive from the essence of man himself and to apply to all of human history. Man's very pretense of having definitively risen above his fallen estate becomes the most grievous testimony to his flawed nature. The possibilities for proximate justice are dependent upon man's recognition of the intrinsic limits of his own resources. Only then does his nature become open to the greatest of ethical resources.

## Foreign Policy: In a State of Nature

Foreign policy is a distinctive domain of political behavior, for it takes place within a state of nature, i.e., in a setting where no one government has a legitimate monopoly on the use of force. In the absence of a world agency that can rule authoritatively on the justified use of force, each state reserves to itself the right to make this judgment, and each sees as a primary obligation preserving its security against outside force. Indeed, this right is the essence of the state's claim to sovereignty. This claim together with the anarchic context gives rise to the most basic ethical issue in foreign policy—the clash between state security and moral norms.

The state's claim to the use of force derives much of its legitimacy from the contention that only through force can it be protected against an even greater use of force and an even greater deprivation of freedom. In this sense, the justification for the state's use of force in foreign policy is similar to the justification for its use in domestic policy. This in turn is an aspect of the justification for the broader claim by the state to safeguard the welfare of the community.

The authority of the United States in foreign affairs derives from the very character of sovereignty itself, and it existed before the Constitution, even before the Declaration of Independence.

Even before the Declaration, the colonies were a unit in foreign affairs, acting through a common agency. . . . Rulers come and go; governments end and forms of government change; but sovereignty survives. A political society cannot endure without a supreme will somewhere. Sovereignty is never held in suspense.[22]

The distinction between the state's authority in domestic affairs and its authority in foreign affairs has major implications not only for the ethical evaluation of foreign policy action but also for the instruments necessary to that action—notably the diplomatic corps, the armed services, and the intelligence arm. If we define the authority of these instruments by the same ethical and legal criteria we apply to the instruments of domestic policy, we sweep aside the radical difference between the realms in which the two originate and operate.

I have argued that reconciliation of the claims of order with those of justice, to the degree that it has been possible in political history, has depended on the acknowledgment by both governors and citizens of a Higher Law that in a social contract defines the rights and duties of both. The most direct prescription for resolving the ethical dilemmas of international politics would be to seek a comparable outcome for the whole world—that is, to define the rights and duties of the citizens of the-world-as-a-whole in their relation with those of a political authority for the-world-as-a-whole. But this parallel to the way in which ethical tensions have been lessened in domestic politics lacks reality for world politics, and from this arise the ethical dilemmas of foreign policy behavior.

Given polities are all to a degree concentric—that is, they are centered about some common core of ethnic or historical or geographical or military experience. That concentration, to be sure, varies enormously in quality and durability. For some it is fragile and evanescent; for others, strong and enduring. International politics as a whole, however, cannot be understood in concentric terms. It is rather an *eccentric* realm—that is, one without a common center. Its many polities, each with a different center, interact outside the context of legitimate authority in an indeterminate fashion with unpredictable consequences. As Paul Ramsey said:

> The political life of mankind goes on perennially under the sign of the verdict of Babel. Politics in every age goes on as if that verdict has not been set aside. It is as if the study of international politics gives knowledge of the life of mankind on the underside of that divine decision.[23]

International politics is the scene of diversity *par excellence*.

Given the deficiencies of international politics, we cannot extend to that arena the arrangements by which particular polities have achieved a tolerable resolution of the claims of justice with those of order. The difficulties of bringing foreign policy behavior into accord with moral norms stem from these deficiencies and from the impossibility of this extension. These difficulties have led to the conclusion, characteristic of the "realist" school, that the guideline for state behavior in foreign affairs must be the national interest; this interest "can only be defined in terms of national security, and national security must be defined as integrity of the national territory and of its institutions."[24] Professor Morgenthau closes his book *In Defense of the National Interest* with this stirring appeal:

> And, above all, remember always that it is not only a political necessity but also a moral duty for a nation to follow in its dealings with other nations but one guiding star, one rule for action: THE NATIONAL INTEREST.[25]

From the perspective of the "realist," empirical distinctions in the actual behavior of states tend to be erased in light of the basic behavioral traits all have in common, and distinctions over the degree to which their behavior accords with moral norms tend to disappear in the face of the single and universal imperative that they pursue the national interest.

## The Drive to Preserve Autonomy

States have, as a matter of fact, assigned first priority to preserving their autonomy. Under exceptional circumstances states may be willing to enter into larger patterns of political association. But these acts of association are deemed legitimate to the degree that the exercise of autonomy makes them possible. There is a universal condemnation of imperialism, defined as the coercive imposition of a state's will upon another state against its will. Indeed, the fundamental ethical issue in international politics can be said to lie in this persistent tension between the claim of autonomy and the drive toward imperialism. But in saying this we must define the term "imperialism" in its generic sense and not restrict it to the relation between a particular group of Western states and the peoples of

Asia or Africa. The earliest, most persistent, most egregious exercises of imperial coercion have been by European rulers against other Europeans.

We cannot equate the preservation of state autonomy with the preservation of moral autonomy, however, because all states, however repressive or unjust, defend their autonomy. We are not even on sure ground in saying that the defense of state autonomy may be justified as a necessary condition of ethical activity. In ethical analysis we must weigh the threat of imperialism against the threat of tyranny—i.e., the cost from the state's loss of its collective autonomy to another state against the toll it exacts upon its own citizens by depriving them of their own autonomy.

We may distinguish four situations: (1) the state is important as a barrier to imperialism without and respects the claims of autonomy within; (2) the state is important as a barrier to imperialism without but violates the claims of autonomy within; (3) the state respects the claims of autonomy within but is indifferent or prejudicial as a barrier to imperialism without; (4) the state violates the claims of autonomy within and is itself a source of imperialism without. (The ethical assessment of the role of human rights in foreign policy is a specific aspect of this general problem.) Ethical judgment is least difficult in cases one and four. Where state autonomy serves as a defense against both imperialism and tyranny, it enjoys the highest legitimacy; where it serves as a shield for both imperialism and tyranny, it is most clearly denied any claim to legitimacy. Ethical judgment is more difficult in the other two cases: where autonomy serves as a barrier to imperialism but as an instrument of tyranny, and where it serves as a barrier to tyranny but is indifferent to, or may become an instrument of, imperialism.

Clearly, one cannot make valid proximate judgments in foreign policy unless one takes into account the qualitative differences in the claims to autonomy—unless, that is, one moves beyond the "realist" tendency to reduce all these claims to the least common denominator of the national interest. And we must recall once again that proximate judgments cannot be made in the absence of precise, detailed, and seasoned knowledge of the internal and external structure and policies of specific states. While imperialism and tyranny can be defined in the abstract, we cannot evaluate the ethical dimension of a given foreign policy without scrupulously assessing how the concepts of imperialism and tyranny apply to it.

## The Periods of Peace

The degree to which a state's foreign policy may approach moral norms is also closely related to the character of the state of nature. The international relations of certain states at certain periods have more nearly resembled those of individuals in Locke's state of nature than those in Hobbes's. Karl Deutsch has described these patterns as "pluralistic security communities" in which states not only have remained at peace for long periods but have had no serious expectations that any one would use force in its relations with any other. A recent related view is Robert Keohane and Joseph Nye's conception of "complex interdependence." Under such circumstances there is a lessening of the general tension between the standards for domestic policy and the standards for foreign policy. Moreover, the specific instruments of statecraft— military, diplomatic, intelligence—can then more justifiably be brought under the constraints applied to the instruments of domestic politics. The degree to which "the vast external realm" approaches a Lockean state of nature is the single most important factor affecting the extent to which foreign policy behavior can be expected to approximate ethical norms.

During periods of peace and moderation, allegiance to a form of higher law seems to obtain among states, and a partial social contract assigns some fairly well-defined rights and duties to each. Such periods, however, have never been universal or durable. The larger pattern of international politics reveals a recurrent attempt by hegemonic states to assert their power over others, and a persistent attempt by threatened states to preserve their autonomy. Neither moral nor legal norms have been sufficient to guarantee independence. Time and time again countervailing power has been necessary to deter the external threat and, where deterrence failed, to to defend the independence of states against it. The balance of power has been essential to state autonomy.

The balance of power has passed through four major historic phases. The first was the *local balance* that prevailed among the Italian city-states during the Renaissance. This system was soon absorbed within the larger *regional balance* of Western Europe, which involved France, Spain, England, and Austria, along with several lesser states.

The third stage may be called the *continental balance,* in which the several regions of Europe came to interact with one another. This system emerged from the Seven Years' War (1756-63), in whose outcome Russia played an important part. It should be noted, however, that the interaction of Western Europe with Eastern Europe brought together two regional systems that had evolved in opposite directions. In the West the principle of autonomy had prevailed over that of hegemony, while in the East hegemony prevailed over autonomy. The balance of power was not, as a *principle,* indigenous to the Russian experience as it was to, say, the British or Dutch.

After the most formidable hegemonic threat in the history of the states system until that time—the Napoleonic Empire—was thrown back, the peacemakers of 1815 seemed able to put the relations among states on a more stable basis than they had been on at any other time since the state system emerged. During the nineteenth century, international politics seemed to correspond more closely than ever to the moderation Locke described. Britain, the world's most influential state, came more and more to see itself as the ally of autonomy in its double sense: protector of the independence of states from external threats and supporter of the internal rights of citizens.

Anglo-American relations provide a notable illustration of the Lockean character of the hundred years of peace that preceded World War I. The two states progressed toward disarmament, legal understandings, the peaceful arbitration of disputes, and the reduction of trade barriers. Better foreign relations were connected significantly with domestic developments, as both states moved toward greater equality in freedom for their people.

Through the extension of these powerful trends in nineteenth-century international politics, Woodrow Wilson sought to transform the character of international politics itself—to make the Lockean order both universal and enduring. But the very event that gave President Wilson the main momentum for his enormous undertaking, the First World War, also registered the emergence of forces that would defeat his aspirations.

World War I signified the breakdown of the classical balance of power, and of the tendencies toward moderation that had rested upon it. Beyond this, it signified the introduction of the new paganism into international politics. By this I mean, referring back to the quotation from Sabine, the reunification of the supreme civil authority and the supreme moral authority in the state—often pointing to the deification of the sovereign's word. Belief in the existence of a Higher Law, which Wilson had hoped would become universal, instead seemed to shrink to ever smaller confines. The century that Wilson had hoped would move steadily toward moderation has instead witnessed a resurgence of conflict reminiscent of the Machiavellian era.

The twentieth century has seen the search for a *global balance,* in the great international struggles—World War I, World War II, the Cold War. The stakes of the struggle have grown enormously. Local, regional, and even continental balances had shifted many times, but these shifts were always parts of a far larger whole. With the emergence of the fourth stage in the balance, the lesser balances came to be absorbed by the larger. Alterations of the global balance hold possibilities of irreversibility that alterations of prior balances could not have had, adding enormously to the difficulty of applying ethical judgments to foreign policy.

## The Impact of Recent Events

The independence and autonomy of the state is threatened by tyranny and imperialism. The Soviet Union is an embodiment of both threats. The primary foreign policy challenge of our time has been the growth and expansion of Soviet power.

That the Soviet Union is tyrannical in its internal structure was clear from its very birth. At that time the Communists deliberately destroyed the possibility that, after the collapse of the tsardom, the Russian people might be able to reconstitute their political life on the basis of a social contract. George Kennan has painted an unforgettable picture of the fateful climax of the 1918 constitutional convention:

> Lenin himself was present, and acted as master of ceremonies for his faction. It was plain to observers that every nerve of his politically impassioned being was aroused by the supreme parliamentary contest. His face deathly pale with tenseness, his burning eyes darting constantly over the scene and absorbing every detail, he directed his cohorts like a commander in battle, whenever there was any chance of dominating the proceedings. When opposition speakers had the floor, he stretched out at full length on the steps leading to the podium and reinforced the harassing operations of his followers by appearing to go to sleep out of sheer boredom.
>
> When it became evident, toward midnight, that the S-R's [Social Revolutionaries] were prepared to drive through, on the strength of their majority in the Assembly, a whole series of independent resolutions having virtual constitutional effect, the Bolsheviki demonstratively walked out on the proceedings. . . . From that moment on, the situation in the hall became very ugly. With no further visible reason for restraint, the armed sailors began to show increasing signs of truculence and impatience. . . . At 4:40 a.m., the session was finally closed under mounting pressure from the sailors. To the accompaniment of a torrent of abuse and menacing shouts from their guardians, the exhausted deputies began to leave the palace. There is no question but that the safety of the entire Assembly hung, at this moment, by the slenderest thread; for the mood of the sailors was by this time such that if a single shot had been fired a massacre would unquestionably have followed. . . .
>
> In tiny groups, the harassed and exhausted deputies disappeared into the darkness of the winter morning and sought whatever places of refuge or hiding they could find in the great snowbound city. . . .
>
> By ten o'clock in the morning, the Soviet government had issued a decree dissolving the Assembly and had barred the doors of the great palace against any re-entry of the deputies.
>
> Thus ended Russia's one and only constitutional convention. . . . From now on, there could be no really established claim to popular sanction on the part of the Soviet regime.[26]

While the tendencies toward tyranny had certain roots in the Russian historical experience, they were greatly reinforced by the Marxist-Leninist approach to politics. Marxism obscures the whole range of problems involved in reconciling order with justice, reducing such problems in the Soviet regime to what it says they are in the "capitalist" world—mere "epiphenomena." The role to which Marxism tries to reduce religion, i.e., to the "opiate of the masses," is the role to which Marxism actually reduces the fundamental questions of justice in the political order.

The ethical bankruptcy of Marxism-Leninism was made clear in one of the most important political documents of our time, Khrushchev's speech denouncing Stalin before the twentieth congress of the Soviet Communist party in 1956:

> Stalin . . . used extreme methods and mass repressions at a time when the Revolution was already victorious, when the Soviet state was strengthened, when the exploiting classes were already liquidated and socialist relations were rooted solidly in all phases of national economy, when our party was politically consolidated and had strengthened itself both numerically and ideologically. . . .
>
> This terror was actually directed not at the remnants of the defeated exploiting classes but against the honest workers of the party and of the Soviet state. . . .
>
> When Stalin said that one or another should be arrested, it was necessary to accept on faith that he was an "enemy of the people." Meanwhile, Beria's gang, which ran the organs of state security, outdid itself in proving the guilt of the arrested and the truth of materials which it falsified. . . . And how is it possible that a person confesses to crimes which he has not committed? Only in one way—because of application of physical methods of pressuring him, tortures, bringing him to a state of unconsciousness, deprivation of his judgment, taking away his human dignity.[27]

The aspect of Khrushchev's speech that most clearly reveals the radical errors of Marxism is his own puzzlement that most tyrannical aspects of Stalinism began only *after* the supposed root of all injustice—the possession of private property—had largely disappeared. When the shallow perversity of this notion is set against the profundity of the Christian understanding of human nature and history, it is clear that Stalinism was not an aberration; it was, rather, a logical outgrowth of Marxist-Leninist assumptions.

The logic of Marxism leads to domestic tyranny and toward imperial expansion. *Pravda* carried a revealing formulation of the Soviet position in its analysis of the 1968 Soviet invasion of Czechoslovakia:

> The anti-socialist elements in Czechoslovakia actually covered up the demand for so-called neutrality and Czechoslovakia's withdrawal from the socialist community with talk about the right of nations to self-determination. However, the implementation of such "self-determination," in other words, Czechoslovakia's detachment from the socialist community, would have come into conflict with its own vital interests and would have been detrimental to the other socialist states. . . . The anti-socialist path, "neutrality," to which the Czechoslovak people were being pushed would bring it to the loss of its national independence. . . . The help to the working people of Czechoslovakia by other socialist countries, which prevented the export of counter-revolution from abroad, constitutes the real sovereignty of the Czechoslovak socialist republic against those who would like to deprive it from its sovereignty and give up the country to imperialism.[28]

In summary, the Soviet Union equates the maintenance of sovereignty and national independence with the maintenance of "socialism"; the degree to which "socialism" is being maintained is to be determined by the Soviet Union; and so the Soviet Union has the sole power to determine the "meaning" of Czechoslovakia's "independence." Under this Brezhnev Doctrine, Moscow will come to the aid of any "socialist" state in trouble. As Vernon Aspaturian has pointed out, this doctrine has now been given a world-wide application, by S.V. Chervonenko among others:

> Chervonenko asserted in connection with the Afghanistan invasion that the Soviet Union "would not permit another Chile"—a rather imperious and arrogant pronouncement in itself—and made the extraordinary statement that now any country, in any region, anywhere on the globe, "has the full right to choose its friends and allies, and if it becomes necessary, to repel them with the threat of counter-revolution or a foreign intervention." This expanded Brezhnev doctrine serves not only to justify the invasion of Afghanistan but also retroactively to justify the Cuban/Soviet military interventions in Angola and on the Horn of

Africa, and it poses an immediate threat to Iran or any other country where internal chaotic conditions can generate "invitations" to Moscow for support to quell internal counter-revolutions or external intervention. Czechoslovakia 1968 and Afghanistan 1979 provide sufficient cause for concern that Soviet leaders are not overly fastidious in examining their invitations and are fully capable of inviting themselves, should no invitation be forthcoming.[29]

To support this globalization of the Brezhnev Doctrine, Moscow has massively increased its strategic and conventional military power. The power of the Soviet Union is now projected globally, particularly through the growth of its navy.

In the face of this challenge, the first responsibility of a morally responsible U.S. foreign policy is to build up the countercoalition that can block the expansion of Soviet power, the primary threat to autonomy in both its external and its internal dimensions.

The formation of such a counterbalance is difficult for four reasons. First, in part because of our policies in World War II, the old European balance, already weakened by the First World War, was smashed. The breakdown produced a situation of strategic, economic, and diplomatic imbalance that persists, with the effect that the Europeans, left to their own initiatives, often show strong tendencies toward one-sided accommodation to Soviet hegemony.

A second factor is the asymmetrical transformation of the Third World. As long as Britain and France could tap their bases of power overseas, they could serve as significant counterweights to the Soviet Union. The anti-colonial revolt has greatly diminished the European colonial presence while leaving the vast Soviet colonial holdings untouched, greatly increasing Soviet power at the expense of the historic European states. This is not to defend the European colonial presence; it is merely to point out that the anti-colonial movement, which is still going on, has adversely affected the global balance.

A third factor is the impact of Marxist thought and Marxist movements, particularly in the Third World. According to Marxist-Leninist propaganda, the threat to autonomy comes from "capitalist imperialism," and the means for checking that threat is the "socialist commonwealth," at whose center, of course, lies the

Soviet Union. In the upside-down world of Marxist propaganda, the aggressor and the defender exchange roles.

The fourth factor is the development of nuclear weapons, which reinforces tendencies toward a one-sided accommodation with the Soviet Union under the assumption that only in this way can nuclear war be averted. The uncritical quest for "peace" works against a policy of balance.

The most profound divergences in U.S. foreign policy concern the relative importance to be assigned to the multiple threats we face. I contend that unless we give highest attention to the containment of Soviet expansion, we will be unable to deal effectively with the other challenges, e.g., those of the Third World, or of arms control. The Soviet Union's projection of its power on a global basis and its deliberate use of terrorism as an instrument of policy (recently documented by Claire Sterling in *The Terror Network*) mean it is impossible to separate Third World problems from Soviet expansionism. Moscow has an increasing capability to make its power felt anywhere in the Third World, and it uses that power to gain objectives that conflict with Western values and interests.

Similar considerations apply to the control of nuclear weapons. Here, as in all other aspects of our relations with the Soviet Union, there can be no "détente" without containment. Whenever Moscow feels the "correlation of forces" is moving in its favor, it will act to accelerate and consolidate that advantage, as its extraordinary strategic build-up under the SALT accords illustrates. A Western counterpoise, far from being in contradiction with effective arms control, is the precondition for it. And arms control is a *political* process—it can result only from an explicit decision of the Soviet Union, whatever the aspirations of those who cherish peace may be. Reduction of the danger of nuclear war can result only from deliberate diplomatic-strategic calculations of states.

## The American Experience

America's historical experience and its situation in world politics today necessarily influence our assessment of what a responsible U.S. foreign policy should be. Throughout most of our history, we have enjoyed the special advantages of an insular position, and this has profoundly influenced the assumptions we make about how to relate ethics to foreign policy. The late Arnold Wolfers expressed a penetrating insight into the difference in experience between the states of Continental Europe and the Anglo-Americans and the effect this has had on how they view the relation between morality and foreign policy:

> While the Continentals were arguing about the dilemma of statesmen faced by the irreconcilable demands of necessity and morality, English and American thinkers in turn were engaged in a debate about the best way to applying accepted principles of morality to the field of foreign policy. Here the assumption was that statesmen and nations enjoyed considerable freedom to choose the right path in their external conduct as they did in their internal policies. . . . This was a philosophy of choice, then, which was bound to be ethical, over against a philosophy of necessity, in which forces beyond moral control were believed to prevail. . . . Whereas the philosophy of necessity tends to lead to resignation, irresponsibility, or even to the glorification of amorality, the philosophy of choice lends itself to excessive moralism and self-righteousness as if the leeway for choice were unlimited and were of the same dimension for all.[30]

Americans' tendency to exaggerate the degree to which foreign policy could be made to conform to ethical norms was reinforced by their enjoyment, for much of their history, of what Vann Woodward has called a remarkable degree of "free security":

> . . . the costly navy that policed and defended the Atlantic was manned and paid for by British subjects for more than a century, while Americans enjoyed the added security afforded without added cost to themselves. In 1861 the United States was maintaining the second largest merchant marine in the world without benefit of a battle fleet. At that time there were only 7,600 men in the United States Navy as compared with more than ten times that number in the British Navy.[31]

America enjoyed "free security" on land as well as water:

> Upon the outbreak of the Civil War the United States Army numbered a few more than sixteen thousand men, and 183 of its 198 companies were spread among seventy-nine posts on the Indian frontier. The remaining fifteen companies were available for "defense" of the Canadian and Atlantic frontiers, and the

incipient Confederate frontier. . . . Military expenditures in the 1880s were never over four-tenths of one per cent of the gross national product.[32]

Woodrow Wilson sought to transform the nature of international politics by moving it toward permanent moderation. The central problems Americans face in world politics may be said to stem from the failure of the Wilsonian vision or, to put it in other terms, from the fact that their nation has now been "continentalized." The United States can no longer escape the ethical complexities of *raison d'état*. Indeed, those problems are now far more troublesome than ever before, for two reasons.

First, we have been plunged, with shattering suddenness, from a position of privileged insularity into an international arena of awesome threats: the new face of totalitarian tyranny and imperialism; an unparalleled expansion of nuclear weapons; the tangled problems of justice and order in the vast Third World, precipitately liberated from prior patterns of governance, often with no accepted system of external or internal legitimacy.

Second, the United States, though in a sense only "born yesterday" to world affairs, now finds itself the keystone of a vital countercoalition against Soviet power and ambition. America's responsibilities are in some ways comparable to those Britain bore in the era of the Pax Britannica, and derive their ethical dimension in part from the fact that the United States protects the autonomy of many other states beside itself. Yet its duties are more onerous than Britain's were then, in part because the tendencies Hobbes described are far more powerful than ever and in part because, as Walter Lippmann once observed, no other state serves as a net under America now, as America served as a net under Britain then.

These radical changes in America's international position should promote searching intellectual and ethical debate.

Let me summarize in six points:

First, although the behavior of all states, particularly in their foreign policy, falls short of the norms of Christian ethics, we still have an obligation to make proximate ethical judgments. The quality of the autonomy states seek to preserve is of central importance to this judgment. In this respect I agree with Raymond Aron:

Between a society that is essentially totalitarian and a society that is essentially liberal, a man who, without being converted to the so-called new faith, chooses the former or sees no real difference between the two has become blind to fundamental values. . . . Our duty is to combat what we condemn and not to assume in advance the privileges of the pure spectator, as if our immediate future were already our distant past. I am the one who is deliberating and not my grandchildren. If they do not take the totalitarian threat as a tragedy, perhaps I may have helped to make their detachment possible by the very fact that I will have averted the danger. But to invoke a future detachment is really to seek an excuse for cowardice or abstention.[33]

Second, in making these proximate judgments, we must try to understand their empirical complexity. We are not entitled, however intense our concern, to substitute sincerity of intention for accuracy of knowledge. To avoid the temptations of the terrible simplifiers we should bear in mind Aristole's great maxim: "Look for precision in each class of things just so far as the nature of the subject admits."[34]

Third, in dealing with the complexities of the external world, the guidelines that govern our domestic policies, based on our constitution and a moral consensus, are insufficient. We must recognize the requirements of an effective balance of power and alliance strategy.

Fourth, to the degree that the state of nature or "real world" fits Locke's view (man has an inherent moral sense and a capacity for social relations and can attain a measure of order and justice outside the state; therefore the sovereign of the state needs and can claim only limited coercive power), the ethical dilemma lessens. We should constantly strive to moderate conflict in the interests of order, justice, and freedom.

Fifth, we must guard against the risks of invoking a double moral standard. The very fact that a society is open to public criticism is evidence of an ethical component in its consensus. To direct our criticism, asymmetrically, against the very societies that make criticism possible is to retard, not further, the prospects for proximate justice.[35]

Finally, we should beware the risks of surrendering our conscience to the deification of "progressive" forces presumed to be inmanent in the historical process. Historical "progress" does not alter the essence of the ethical problem, which is rooted in man's corruption of his precious gift of freedom. That problem is centered neither in history nor in society. A Christian understanding of the ethical problem reminds us that all ages are equidistant from eternity.

# Religion, Schools, and the Community of Values

TIMOTHY L. SMITH

IN THE YEAR 1741 THE Reverend Theodore Schneider arrived in Pennsylvania to become priest of the tiny flock of German Catholics who had gathered at Goshenhoppen, in what is now Washington township, Berks county. Schneider, 41, was a graduate of the Jesuit seminary at Liège in Belgium and had taught theology and philosophy at the University of Heidelberg, serving one year as rector there. He gave up this promising career to accept an assignment from a missionary society founded specifically to nurture the religious life of Roman Catholics who were making their way to the American frontier.

The residence that Schneider's poor parishioners furnished him was a two-storied house whose ground floor served as a chapel on Sundays and a parish school during the rest of the week. Though outwardly the school seemed traditional enough, it differed in many subtle ways from the parish schools of Europe. Like thousands founded later, this Catholic parochial school owed much to the initiative of families recently settled in new communities who felt a deep need for the sense of belonging and of personal identity that the practice of their common faith supplied. The school rested on an awareness that those who shared this bond of

*Timothy L. Smith is professor of history at the Johns Hopkins University in Baltimore. He has a Ph.D. from Harvard. He is the author of "Revivalism and Social Reform on the Eve of the Civil War" and "Called Unto Holiness," a social history of religion, education, and immigration in the United States.*

faith were not and perhaps never would be a majority in the place to which they had come. It trained children not only to cherish the religion of the Old World but to seize the social and economic opportunities of the New. And the school provided much of the moral and social education that children in an Old World parish gained through informal family and village associations.

In these respects Schneider's school was not much different from those that Protestant congregations of all sorts established soon after they settled in the Pennsylvania wilderness. In Philadelphia and some other places, the Society of Friends occupied a dominant political, social, and economic position. Accordingly, Quakers assumed responsibility for the schooling of not only their own children but also those from families of other faiths who were unable to provide for their youngsters themselves. And in nearby Germantown, for a time, the far-sighted Mennonite Francis Daniel Pastorius maintained a school that he hoped would draw together what he described as "a veritable Noah's Ark of different faiths." His school and community were America's first miniature melting pot, though his aim was to knit Germans of many backgrounds into one community rather than to make them Englishmen.

Generally, however, a more exclusively denominational program of parochial education prevailed among Pennsylvania Protestants regardless of whether their traditions were those of a "state church" or of a "sect." The increasing migration from Germany soon made the back-country west of Philadelphia a kaleidoscope of denominations. Neighborhoods dominated by one church emerged only slowly, as one or another group of settlers proved the better farmers and bought up the land of others nearby. In general, the sectarians—as the Mennonites, Dunkers, and Amish were called—established churches and schools with the least difficulty. They had been first on the ground, and talented and educated leaders had come over from Europe with them. Moreover, they had learned in the Old World the value of group discipline and intimate fellowship for a mobile minority dependent upon one another's loyalty and support.

What resulted in Pennsylvania in the eighteenth century, as later in both the pioneer Midwest and the immigrant neighborhoods of twentieth-century cities, was a society in which religious pluralism was the condition and religious initiative the key to the teaching of children. I have lingered a bit over the Pennsylvania story because I believe it provides a clearer introduction to the tangled history of American education than the better-known chronicle of New England's early schools.

The ethnic and religious homogeneity of colonial New England was not typical of the rest of America at any period. Nor did our modern system of tax-supported education emerge directly out of Puritan law and custom, though later it drew heavily upon them. It was constructed rather in every state and community upon earlier private or denominational efforts. James P. Wickersham's history of education in Pennsylvania, which few now read, clearly shows that this was true of the Quaker commonwealth. Variations on the theme dominate the story of education in Minnesota, Louisiana, New York, Texas, and wherever else cultural and religious diversity was the rule.

## Two Traditions in Public Education

The American system of what nineteenth-century educators called "common schools" stemmed from efforts to harmonize religious conflict by agreement on a set of biblical values rather than from an ideal situation in which conflict did not exist. This is why champions of both parochial and public schools have been able with such apparent logic to appeal to history for proof that theirs is the authentic American tradition. The fact is that we have two authentic American traditions in public education, one religious and the other and more recent one secular. Their history, philosophy, and practice are at no point easily disentangled, precisely because both grew out of pressing social needs.

The prominent position that Protestants of Puritan background held in social and economic life throughout most of the country during the 1800s made it easier for them to accept and indeed sponsor the establishment of state-supported and non-sectarian schools. They were able to control the appointment of teachers and superintendents, acting sometimes, perhaps unconsciously, for their own religious purposes as well as for a democratic society's educational needs.

Yet Roman Catholics, Lutherans, Mormons, and many smaller Protestant denominations found that the system of local support and control, so sacred to American tradition, also lent itself to their purposes. Whenever they were able to establish a religiously homogeneous community, the "public school" inevitably reflected the values and beliefs of the congregation to which most of the people belonged. Thus we find Minnesota Catholics who settled in Archbishop John Ireland's agricultural communities rejoicing at the papal reprieve that allowed them to send their children to the public school when no alternative was available. They saw neither point nor profit in establishing a parish school when virtually everyone in the community, from the school board down, was a devout Catholic. The same was true in many Lutheran communities in the upper Midwest, and in Mormon Utah.

In the cities after 1880, the tide of immigration flowed increasingly from new sources—southern and eastern Europe. Large numbers of Italians, Finns, Poles, and Slavs came to America, along with more than a million Polish and Russian Jews. The whole drama of parochial education was played out again, only this time in an urban and industrial setting rather than an agrarian one.

The older communities of German Jews, for example, were by then well rooted in American soil. They had given up separate day schools in the 1850s and had developed instead an extensive system of Sunday schools to teach their youngsters Jewish law and lore. They proposed to Americanize the children of the new East European immigrants in these Sunday schools, and launched in addition a broad program of charitable "industrial" education.

The Jewish newcomers resisted this calculated Americanization, however, notwithstanding its Jewish sponsorship. They organized instead fraternal associations based on old-country ties and worshiped in hundreds of tiny store-front synagogues in the immigrant sections of New York, Philadelphia, Chicago, and other cities. They first established in connection with these the traditional *hadarim*, tiny one-room schools for teaching religion, but later developed the more professional Talmud Torahs, with graded

classes. Both poverty and eager ambition lay behind their early
decision to operate these schools during hours when the public
schools were not in session so that their children could have the
benefit of both. What followed makes up the most successful
Americanization story in our nation's history. The Jews of New
York and other cities became staunch allies of public, as opposed
to parochial, schools. (On this point, some of their leaders have
recently been trying their best to Americanize the rest of us.)

These and many other aspects of the story of religion in American education are worth telling at much greater length for their
own sake, I believe. It is a pity that the necessity of debating the
issues this question provokes today has so complicated emotions
that to attempt to recreate the story as it actually happened is to
arouse suspicions of special pleading. Perhaps, however, a histo-
rian's first duty is to lay out facts that contradict the myths upon
which so much public argument is based.

The present controversy seems to stem from the conjunction in
our time of three long-term tendencies. One is the increasing pace
of urbanization, which has brought millions of rural Protestants
whose memories are entwined around the village church and
school face to face with the cultural and religious diversity that has
long flourished in American cities. Meanwhile, within all our urban
subcultures, the acceleration of personal and family mobility, both
geographic and social, has disrupted the congregational life of the
ethnic communities whose parochial schools have for decades
symbolized their version of the American way. Finally, the ex-
panded breadth and length of schooling required for success in a
complex industrial society has taxed parish and denominational
resources to the breaking point. The reasons for the controversy,
then, are clear; but the arguments that characterize it are not.

### The Myth of Social Neglect

One of the confusing myths is that church-sponsored schools
have provided only a traditional, classical curriculum, to the great
neglect of the social and vocational needs of children. Many facts
indicate otherwise.

Consider, for example, the preoccupation of Quaker and Moravian schoolmasters in early America with education for the practical affairs of life. William Penn's Frame of Government for Pennsylvania required that every child be taught a useful trade. The famous illustrated reader *The Visible World*, published by the Moravian John Amos Comenius in the seventeenth century, is important not only for its emphasis upon visual images of concrete human and natural objects but also for a long section—some one hundred pages and ninety-eight pictures—describing the arts and crafts of home, field, shop, government, war, and commerce. Later, Protestant and Roman Catholic mission schools for Indians invariably combined literary with vocational training and had as a primary objective the Indian youth's adjustment to the conditions of civilized life. Meanwhile, the Protestant denominational academies of the pioneer Midwest, which were the first to provide schooling beyond the three R's to the frontiersmen's children, were thoroughly saturated with vocationalism.

After the Civil War, the needs of freed Negroes and new immigrants provoked similar responses. General Samuel C. Armstrong put into practice at Hampton Institute a program of agricultural and industrial education fashioned after one his father had developed at a mission school in Hawaii. Booker T. Washington later adapted this program to his purposes at Tuskegee.

In the festering slums of New York, Philadelphia, Boston, and Chicago, organizations like the Protestant Children's Aid Society, the Catholic Society of St. Vincent de Paul, and the Hebrew Free School Association sponsored scores of industrial schools for the children of poor immigrants. Church women in many cases led the way in the formation of kindergartens in which child-centered rather than subject-centered teaching was the rule. Institutional churches and social settlement houses later picked up these ideas and promoted their adoption in the public schools, over the bitter opposition of school superintendents and teachers who were wedded to the rituals of rote memory.

From this parentage, I believe, the progressive movement in American education was born at the end of the nineteenth century. One can learn more about its origins from the labors of social workers than from those of public school officials—more, indeed, from the careers of missionary teachers and pastors. Such persons were in intimate daily contact with the social disorganization that threatened common life among immigrants to the cities, as well as among whites and Negroes scattered across the poor farms and mill towns of the South. The philosophy of the movement they instituted was permeated during the early years with a fervently religious spirit.

Seen in this light, the leadership that private and church schools have recently given to the campaign for higher academic standards may reflect among other things the fact that, dependent as these schools are upon voluntary support, they simply respond to new needs more quickly than the legally and financially entrenched public school system. Long before the first Soviet triumphs in space technology, the sponsors of these schools believed the nation needed a revival of intellectual vigor in the education of children, not just as an ideal but as a practical matter. At any rate, it seems obvious that few judgments helpful to a resolution of our present controversies can be made on the basis of the false belief that only the public and secular system can be counted upon to make the child's social and vocational needs, and those of society, central.

## The Myth of Secularism

Equally great confusion has stemmed from the myth that the system of tax-supported schools established in mid-nineteenth-century America was essentially and necessarily secular in character. A much more accurate description would call it a Protestant nonsectarian system, though this designation, too, would be subject to numerous local variations.

We could learn much from careful studies of the sponsorship of the campaigns that brought public schools into existence in the various states, and of the social and religious backgrounds of the superintendents and teachers who first took charge of them. An old legend, cultivated more or less actively by both defenders and opponents of explicitly secular schooling, has it that anticlerical radicals similar to the feminist agitator Frances Wright deserve much credit for the educational awakening of Horace Mann's day. However, many crucial battles were fought and won by men like Calvin Stowe in Ohio and Calvin Wiley in North Carolina, two whose spiritual lineage is evident from their Christian names. The first state school superintendents in the Middle West were almost all either Protestant ministers or ministers' sons. And the teachers whom local school boards recruited were mostly products of the academies and colleges that the churches had maintained across the preceding decades.

Mann himself sought to remove from the public school classrooms only those evangelical exercises and teachings that he and other Unitarians found objectionable. He did not object to the reading of the Bible. Methodists, as it happened, took the same position—partly, no doubt, because up until that time they too had been a religious minority.

What the men of that age rejected, both in the public schools and, to a surprising degree, in the relations among the denominations themselves, was sectarianism. Rarely, however, did the circle of nonsectarianism stretch far enough to include Jews and Roman Catholics. The school systems of cities both large and small were in fact instruments of an informal Protestant establishment. In a society weighted so heavily toward the Protestant side in wealth and numbers and traditions, little conscious effort was required to make them so.

Later, to be sure, many leaders of the progressive movement in American education acted to minimize or eliminate the more obvious symbols of the commitment of public schools to the majority religious tradition. But the reformers did not end the preeminence of the Protestant middle class in public education. They were themselves representatives of that class. Indeed, the ideology of the progressivism that they sought to impose on the schools in the period before 1920 required scant revision of the traditional framework of values we usually label "Puritan." It called rather for the adoption of methods of instruction calculated to help those values take root among alien peoples who were crowding into the cities and factory towns.

Comprehending these facts is prerequisite to understanding the nature and extent of the change that has taken place in American public education since the First World War. Our present controversy springs not so much from nineteenth-century conflicts as from a quite contemporary encounter between a recently secularized school system and the persistence of traditional religious belief. Home and church and school remain closely interwoven in the perceptions and the affections of a great many American citizens.

## The Myth of Alien Loyalties

A third myth alleges that priests and lay teachers in immigrant communities have perpetuated parochial schools in order to retard the Americanization of their youngsters. Dealing with this legend raises a whole series of questions about the meaning of "Americanization" and the usefulness of alternative terms such as acculturation, assimilation, and cultural pluralism. But such questions do not really seem of fundamental importance, in the light of repeated demonstrations that most of the newcomers were committed to becoming Americans by the very act of their migration from the Old World. To be sure, each ethnic group had to work out for itself the basic alterations in patterns of custom and belief that life in the United States required. The result, however, was a new institutional and ideological framework, adjusted in numerous ways to a social and economic order in which the members of the group had at first been strangers.

Parish schools, which from the viewpoint of outsiders seemed bent upon binding the children of immigrants to outmoded traditions, were in fact prime agents of this process of adjustment. In such schools, the teacher's close association with both the family and the church helped make his or her contribution effective. Such a teacher understood better than others the dismay of the elders when children moved so fast as to cut their own parents out of their circle. And at the point of threatened rupture, the teacher often acted to hold the generations together, even at the cost of delaying some aspects of the children's adjustment.

The alternative was a determined effort by outside agencies to wrench the children loose from their cultural roots. In many cases, the absence of a well-developed immigrant community gave this choice the field. But looking backward, who, on humane grounds alone, would have elected it? Many public school systems flatly rejected it. The real point at issue, it soon became clear, was whether America's social values and personal standards were to be determined by granting as wide as possible freedom and initiative to groups and individuals, or by allowing a dominant elite to fashion within broad limits a single moral design for all, and to give those who conducted the public schools the power to execute it.

## The Myth of Wholly Separate Funding

Finally, and what will be most disturbing to many, one cannot find in the history of American education much support for the notion that our oldest traditions are violated whenever public funds are used in support of private or parochial schools.

For many years after 1800, for example, the state of New York distributed public school funds to parish institutions willing to undertake the free education of poor children. Methodist, Baptist, Anglican, and Friends schools all enjoyed this bounty at one time or another. The Jewish synagogue in 1813 asked the legislature to include its school as well, conveying the message through the great Jeffersonian DeWitt Clinton, who was then mayor of New York City and later became governor of the state. Clinton was head of the Public School Society, a private association that gradually won a monopoly of the privilege of educating the city's poor, partly through stressing its nonsectarian piety.

In 1840, Roman Catholic Archbishop John Hughes complained of the Protestant character of the religious training offered in the Society's schools—still the only free public schools in New York City—and asked for a separate subsidy for Catholic institutions. Governor William H. Seward supported the request, out of profound concern for the welfare of the state. The Protestant outcry was so great as to destroy any chance of success for the proposal.

The spirited bishop then joined the governor in forcing through the legislature a bill forbidding the distribution of state funds to any private or parochial schools.

The principle was not observed, however, nor is it likely that Archbishop Hughes or his successors wished it to be. True, the city of New York organized a public school system, pursuant to the law. But after the Civil War, Catholic, Protestant, and Jewish industrial schools in the city received continuous subsidies for teaching poor youngsters the minimal curriculum that the state required. The practice did not end until the close of the nineteenth century.

The justification for these repeated compromises lay in what many believed was a state of educational emergency. From the Civil War onward there were never schoolrooms enough in New York to accommodate all the city's children. And the deficiency increased every time an immigrant ship docked at Castle Island. Meanwhile, among Negroes and mountain whites in the South, what seemed like herculean efforts by church and philanthropic agencies had not done much to combat illiteracy there, either.

In the summer of 1883, some of the country's most prominent clergymen and educators gathered at the Methodist camp meeting grounds in Ocean Grove, New Jersey, to plead with the national congress for passage of the Blair Bill. This measure proposed to give federal aid to the common schools of states and territories in proportion to the statistics of illiteracy revealed by the census of 1880. Speakers noted that the churches and benevolent societies had waged a long crusade for the education of freedmen, Indians, and immigrants; yet the illiteracy rate was rising in the very areas where the local communities had seemingly reached the limit of their resources. The only sure, equitable solution was federal aid.

Though the Blair Bill did not pass, the debate over it focused public attention on the crisis. In succeeding years state tax funds continued to find their way, sometimes by devious routes, into the treasuries of private and church-related schools. Conversely, private funds often subsidized the tax-supported schools, particularly those serving blacks in the South and children in poorer sections of the growing cities. Many reforms of the public schools in the progressive era—including kindergartens, instruction in manual

arts and domestic science, school nurses, and school lunches—
were initiated with private funds before they were accepted in the
public budget.

The intertwining of public and private support has not ceased in
our day. In the state of Texas, for example, orphanages sponsored
by Baptists, Churches of Christ, and other denominations receive
aid from state school funds in the same generous proportions as do
public schools. This is done legally by the simple expedient of
organizing a school district whose boundaries coincide with those
of the orphanage property. Other examples involving both Catholics and Protestants could be cited for nearly every state.

## The Promise of the Future

One can scarcely hope, therefore, to find in the history of American education any abiding principle or inviolate tradition upon
which to base a resolution of the present disagreements. Nor does
there appear to be a consistent set of precedents in constitutional
law. The voting public, like the courts, will have to thrash the whole
matter out according to what seems rational, expedient, and
humane. Perhaps it is too much to hope—but we should nevertheless continue to hope—that alternative solutions will be judged
according to the welfare of the nation and its children, not the
vested interests of either the public or the religious and private
school systems. Both sets of systems have now achieved highly
institutionalized national organizations. Vested bureaucratic and
professional interests dominate both, belying the talk of parish, of
family, of community control. And both, it seems to me, are
pressed by the inner logic of their institutional development to
make the interests and needs of children secondary to other considerations.

It would be a pity if one day historians could fairly conclude that
American education in the twentieth century passed through three
stages: the subject-centered, the student-centered, and, at last, the
system-centered. Let us hope, rather, that within both the public
and the parochial educational empires, a humane and thoughtful
minority of teachers and administrators will strive to reawaken an

older and more ethical tradition in which children were central and their need for a widely shared framework of values not prostituted to partisan advantage. In a meeting of minds among such a moral minority, it seems to me, lies the promise of the future.

In recent years, however, a new barrier to that meeting of minds has emerged, namely, the ethnic and political purposes that have in some cases fueled the movement for private schools.

During the years of bitter initial white reaction to the decisions of the Supreme Court in 1957 calling for the desegregation of public education, we read almost daily of one recalcitrant group or another organizing a private school, usually under church sponsorship, and making its segregationist purposes explicit. To be sure, we understood that denominations such as the Seventh-Day Adventists, the Lutheran Church–Missouri Synod, and the Associate Reformed Presbyterians, as well as the Roman Catholic Church, had long maintained parochial schools for fundamentally moral and religious reasons. And most of us honored the equally long tradition that lay behind the country's denominational colleges, both Protestant and Catholic. But the racially motivated new elementary and secondary schools were of a different character. That they borrowed the rhetoric of patriotism to advance their goals only reminded us that in the 1920s the Ku Klux Klan had used precisely the same tactic. By the 1970s, the sponsors of these new "private" schools had merged the rhetoric of right-wing politics with appeals for the protection of moral values in presenting their claims for public subsidies, tax exemptions, and tuition credits. I, for one, am not persuaded that the social hostility and reactionary political ideals their founders voiced only twenty-five years ago have given way to a primary concern for the preservation of humane values.

Nevertheless, whether standing in a presumed majority or minority, moral persons now have a chance to unite in setting forth some pervasive ideals that all parties can find historical, rational, and ethical grounds to affirm. It is madness to suppose that the rights of individuals can be protected only by the paralyzing of a society's power to name and sustain what constitutes goodness, truth, and love. The degree to which moral concerns, and the human welfare they nurture, truly govern those of us who may choose to unite in proclaiming such ideals will be measured by our willingness to strip away the veils of special privilege, of political intention, and of social prejudice that hide us from one another, and from our own best selves.

In short, those of us who consider ourselves champions of the public schools ought now to support every compromise of policy that is not a clear and immediate threat to the constitutional guarantee of the free exercise of our several faiths and of our freedom from the establishment of any one of them. The warning that such accommodation might set in motion irresistible tendencies toward more basic compromises of principle is an argument from fear. It denies the faith in democratic processes that liberals profess, and harks back to many a historic polemic against necessary change. Moreover, it ignores the fact that a large number of the Catholic and Protestant laypersons who are now involved in promoting parochial or private schools, perhaps a majority, believe deeply in the separation of church and state. In matters of religious conflict, all of us should long since have learned that rigidity begets only reaction, and intransigence only spite.

# Notes

## The Changing Catholic Scene
### JAMES V. SCHALL, S.J.

1. Flannery O'Connor, *The Habit of Being: The Letters of Flannery O'Connor* (New York: Viking, 1979), p. 422.

2. Heinrich Rommen, "The Church and Human Rights," in R. Caponigri, ed., *Modern Catholic Thinkers* (New York: Harper Torchbooks, 1960), 2:391.

3. Cf. the author's "Culture and Human Rights," *America*, January 7, 1978.

4. Cf. address of John Paul II to UNESCO, June 2, 1980.

The primary and essential task of culture in general, and also of all culture, is education. Education consists in fact in enabling man to become more man, to "be" more and not just to "have" more and consequently, through everything he "has," everything he possesses, to "be" man more fully. For this purpose, man must be able to "be more" not only "with others," but also "for others." Education is of fundamental importance for the formation of inter-human and social relations. Here too I touch upon a set of axioms on the basis of which the traditions of Christianity that have sprung from the Gospel meet the educative experience of so many well-disposed and deeply wise men, so numerous in all centuries of history. In our age too, there is no lack of them, of these men who reveal themselves as great, simply through their humanity which they are able to share with others, in particular with the young. At the same time, the symptoms of crisis of all kinds to which there succumb environments and societies which are among those best-off in other ways—crises which affect above all young generations—vie with each other in bearing witness that the work of man's education is not carried out only with the help of institutions, with the help of organized and material means, however excellent they may be. They also show that the most important thing is always man, man and his moral authority which comes from the truth of his principles and from the conformity of his actions with these principles [John Paul II, UNESCO Address, *Osservatore Romano*, English edition, June 23, 1980, p. 10].

5. John Paul II, Address of February 17, 1981, *Osservatore Romano*, English edition, February 23, 1981, p. 6.

6. John Paul II, Address of January 28, 1979, III.2, from *Puebla: A Pilgrimage of Faith* (Boston: St. Paul Editions, 1979), p. 115.

7. Cf. Charles N. R. McCoy, *The Structure of Political Thought* (New York: McGraw-Hill, 1963), chapter 6; Leo Strauss, *Natural Right and History* (Chicago: University of Chicago, 1952).

8. Cf. Herbert Deane, *Political and Social Ideas of St. Augustine* (New York:

107

Columbia, 1963); Christopher Dawson, "St. Augustine and His Age," in *St. Augustine* (New York: Meridian, 1957), pp. 11-78.

9. Cf. the author's "Old Testament and Political Theory," *The Homiletic and Pastoral Review*, November 1979, pp. 64-72.

10. Romans 13:2-6. Cf. also Oscar Cullmann, *The State in the New Testament* (New York: Scribner's, 1958); Heinrich Schlier, "The State According to the New Testament," in *The Relevance of the New Testament* (New York: Herder, 1968), pp. 215-38.

11. Cf. Charles H. McIlwain, *The Growth of Political Thought in the West* (New York: Macmillan, 1932). Cf. also the author's *Christianity and Politics* (Boston: St. Paul Editions, 1981), chapter 3.

12. Cf. A. Woznicki, *A Christian Humanism: Karol Wojtyla's Existential Personalism* (New Britain, Conn.: Mariel, 1980).

13. Cf. Stanley Jaki, *The Road of Science and the Ways to God* (Chicago: University of Chicago, 1978).

14. Carl Becker, *The Heavenly City of the Eighteenth Century Philosophers* (New Haven: Yale University, 1932). Cf. the author's "From Catholic 'Social Doctrine' to the Kingdom of God on Earth," *Communio*, Winter 1976, pp. 284-300.

15. *Ibid.*, pp. 30, 31.

16. Cf. Robert Nisbet, *History of the Idea of Progress* (New York: Basic Books, 1980).

17. Cf. E. E. Y. Hales, *The Catholic Church in the Modern World* (Garden City, N.Y.: Doubleday Image, 1960), chapters 2-5.

18. Hannah Arendt, *On Revolution* (New York: Viking, 1963).

19. Cf. Norman Macrae, "Must Japan Slow?," *The Economist*, London, "Survey," February 23, 1980. Cf. also the author's forthcoming *Liberation Theology* (San Francisco: Ignatius Press).

20. Cf. Roger Heckel, *Religious Freedom: Texts of John Paul II* (Rome: Pontifical Commission on Justice and Peace, 1980).

21. See "Cuba's Challenge," *Maryknoll*, August 1980, for an example of a Catholic attempt at least to bless the Cuban experiment.

22. See effort to justify Mao in *Holy Cross Quarterly* 7 (1975), nos. 1-4.

23. Cf. Jacques Maritain, "End of Machiavellianism," in J. Evans and L. Ward (eds.), *The Social and Political Philosophy of Jacques Maritain* (Notre Dame: University of Notre Dame, 1976), pp. 292-325.

24. Cf. John Courtney Murray, S.J., *We Hold These Truths* (Garden City, N.Y.: Doubleday Image, 1964); Jacques Maritain, *Man and the State* (Chicago: University of Chicago, 1951), chapter 6. Cf. also Vatican II's "Declaration on Religious Freedom."

25. J. M. Bochenski, *Philosophy—An Introduction* (New York: Harper Torchbooks, 1972) p. 100.

26. Cf. Henri de Saint-Simon, "New Christianity," *Social Organization, the*

*Science of Man, and Other Writings* (New York: Harper Torchbooks, 1952), pp. 81-116.

27. Dale Vree, review of Arthur McGovern, S.J., *Marxism: An American Christian Perspective*, in *New Oxford Review*, April 1981, p. 28.

28. "The Pastoral Letter of 1919," in *The National Pastorals of the American Hierarchy, 1792-1919* (Washington: National Catholic Welfare Conference, 1923), pp. 322, 323.

29. Cf. G. Girardi, *Cristianesimo, Liberazione Umana, Lotta di Classe* (Assisi: Citadella, 1972).

30. Cf. Richard Mulcahy, *The Economics of Heinrich Pesch* (New York: Holt, 1952).

31. Cf. Michael Novak, *Toward a Theology of the Corporation* (Washington: American Enterprise Institute, 1981).

32. Cf. J. Messner, *Social Ethics* (St. Louis: Herder, 1952), p. 214 ff.

33. Cf. Hilaire Belloc, *The Servile State* (New York: Holt, 1946; reissued by Liberty Classics, 1977).

34. E. F. Schumacher, *Small Is Beautiful* (New York: Harper, 1973).

# Legislating Morality: The Role of Religion

## DAVID LITTLE

1. See Jerry Falwell, *Listen, America!* (Garden City, N.Y.: Doubleday, 1980), especially pp. 53, 54. Falwell is anything but crystal clear on this matter, though he appears to support freedom of religion. The distinction he makes between the separation of church and state, in which he believes, and the "separation of God and government," in which he does not believe, is to my knowledge nowhere spelled out.

Falwell appears at one point to go back on his commitment to separation of church and state, at least in public education. "Until about thirty years ago . . . Christian education and the precepts of the Bible still permeated the curriculum of public schools. . . . But our public schools no longer teach Christian ethics . . . " (p. 205). He is of course decrying this state of affairs and apparently would reverse it if he could.

2. *Ibid.*, p. 253.

3. *Ibid.*, p. 201.

4. *Ibid.*, pp. 259, 260.

5. Oxford: Oxford University Press, 1959; reprinted in 1965.

6. Ronald Dworkin, "Liberty and Moralism," in *Taking Rights Seriously* (Cambridge: Harvard University, 1977), pp. 240-58.

7. *Ibid.*, p. 247.

8. As is well known, Roger Williams was not an entirely stable Baptist. He appears to have held his belief in adult baptism by immersion for a short time, on his way toward more radical religious beliefs. Still, the church formed at

Providence by Williams and his fellow refugees seems to have been the first Baptist church in America, and, consequently, Rhode Island became a base of operation and expansion for the Baptists (see Sydney E. Ahlstrom, *A Religious History of the American People* [New Haven: Yale University, 1972], pp. 166-83).

Falwell's connection with the Rhode Island Baptist church is obviously remote. He has even split off from the Southern Baptist denomination. My reference to their both being Baptists is mainly for rhetorical purposes. But whether or not Falwell claims Williams, he should!

9. Although Roger Williams has often been oversold as the founder of religious liberty in this country and has incorrectly been identified with Thomas Jefferson and James Madison with respect to religious pluralism, he is equally ill served if we underrate his significance in the "American experiment." On matters of religion and society, he is in many ways a more interesting figure than Thomas Jefferson, and his achievements in Rhode Island, considering the countervailing pressures of the period, were noteworthy. "Conceived in Puritan 'heresy' and maturing as a remarkable seat of religious pluralism, [Rhode Island] provides both an invaluable insight into the 'left wing' of the Puritan movement and an important anticipation of later American problems and solutions" (Ahlstrom, *op. cit.*, p. 166).

10. *Complete Writings of Roger Williams* (New York: Russell and Russell, 1963), 4:360.

11. *Ibid.*, 7:183.

12. *Ibid.*, 3:358.

13. *Ibid.*, 4:365.

14. *Ibid.*, 3:398, 399.

15. *Ibid.*, 3:398.

16. *Ibid.*, 4:406.

17. I wish to stress that it does not follow from Williams's views that Christians ought to withdraw from civil society. Williams certainly did not withdraw from public affairs in Rhode Island. He would undoubtedly have held that religious people should be free to work out the connections between religious and civil society in their own ways, as long as they extend the same privilege to others.

18. Williams, *op. cit.*, 7:243.

19. See Edmund S. Morgan, *Roger Williams: The Church and the State* (New York: Harcourt, Brace, and World, 1967), pp. 134, 135.

20. Dworkin, *op. cit.*, p. 254.

21. *Ibid.*, p. 254, n. 3.

22. Falwell, *op. cit.*, p. 182.

23. *Ibid.*, p. 184.

24. There is much more to be said on this aspect of the argument than I have supplied. For one thing, we need to attend to the specific role of the courts, as distinct from the legislatures, in resolving questions of public morality. There is currently a deep conflict in our society over this issue, and it requires careful and expert attention. My amateur view is that the courts, in their own way, and probably less self-consciously than is desirable, come up reflecting their own version of consensus on questions of public morality. In theory, it is not, I believe, a bad idea to balance one way of registering consensus with another. Whether in

reference to specific questions like abortion things are now "out of balance," I am not prepared to say.

25. Perry Miller, *Roger Williams: His Contribution to the American Tradition* (New York: Atheneum, 1962), p. 254.

26. John Courtney Murray, S.J., *We Hold These Truths* (Garden City, N.Y.: Doubleday, 1969), especially pp. 64-75.

## Ethics, Power, and U.S. Foreign Policy
### WHITTLE JOHNSTON

1. From text in William Y. Elliott and N. A. McDonald, *Western Political Heritage* (New York: Prentice-Hall, 1949), p. 191.

2. Reinhold Niebuhr, *The Children of Light and the Children of Darkness* (New York: Scribner's, 1944), p. 9.

3. Carl J. Friedrich (ed.), *The Philosophy of Kant* (New York: Modern Library, 1949), pp. 197, 198.

4. Jean Jacques Rousseau, *The Social Contract* (New York: Oxford, 1947), pp. 8, 9.

5. Elliott and McDonald, *op. cit.,* p. 633.

6. Cited in Hans J. Morgenthau, *Politics in the Twentieth Century* (Chicago: University of Chicago, 1962), 3:71.

7. *Ibid.*

8. Elliott and McDonald, *op. cit.,* p. 625.

9. *Ibid.,* p. 626.

10. Call to Conference on Christianity and Politics, Ethics and Public Policy Center, Washington, D.C., May 8-9, 1981.

11. Arnold Wolfers and L. Martin (eds.), *The Anglo-American Tradition in Foreign Affairs* (New Haven: Yale University, 1956), p. 143.

12. Quoted in George Sabine, *A History of Political Theory* (New York: Holt, 1937), p. 609

13. *Ibid.,* p. 139.

14. Elliott and McDonald, *op. cit.,* p. 625.

15. Hans J. Morgenthau, *Scientific Man vs. Power Politics* (Chicago: University of Chicago, 1946), pp. 198, 199.

16. Ernest W. Lefever (ed.), *Ethics and World Politics: Four Perspectives* (Baltimore: Johns Hopkins University, 1972), p. 60.

17. Sabine, *op. cit.,* p. 361.

18. *Ibid.,* p. 369.

19. *Ibid.,* p. 196.

20. Lefever, *op. cit.,* pp. 70, 71.

21. Hedley Bull, *The Anarchical Society* (New York: Columbia University, 1977), pp. 4, 5.

22. Henry Steele Commager (ed.), *Documents of American History* (New York: Appleton-Century-Crofts, 1943), 2:543, 544.

23. Lefever, *op. cit.,* p. 53.

24. Hans J. Morgenthau, *Politics Among Nations,* 4th ed. (New York: Knopf, 1967), p. 542.

25. Hans J. Morgenthau, *In Defense of the National Interest* (New York, Knopf, 1951), p. 242.

26. George F. Kennan, *Russia Leaves the War* (New York: Atheneum, 1967), pp. 350, 352.

27. Hillman M. Bishop and Samuel Hendel (eds.), *Basic Issues of American Democracy,* 5th ed. (New York: Appleton-Century-Crofts, 1965), pp. 495-99.

28. Adda B. Bozeman, *The Future of Law in a Multicultural World* (Princeton: Princeton University, 1971), pp. 187-93.

29. Vernon Aspaturian, "Soviet Global Power and the Correlation of Forces," *Problems of Communism,* May-June 1980, p. 17.

30. Wolfers and Martin, *op. cit.,* pp. xx, xxi.

31. C. V. Woodward, "The Age of Reinterpretation," *The American Historical Review,* October 1960, pp. 4, 5.

32. *Ibid.*

33. Raymond Aron, *Peace and War* (New York: Praeger, 1966), pp. 670, 671.

34. We should all keep in mind Charles Burton Marshall's distinction between a cynic and a skeptic:

A cynic shrugs off differences between right and wrong as merely conventional—a sham, as it were A skeptic acknowledges such differences as real, but regards them to be often complex and subtle, and refuses to arrive at judgments on the basis of declaratory evidence only. Cynicism goes hand in hand with ennui. Skepticism kindles the critical spirit. Every one of us should be skeptical about foreign policy, because that attitude is what helps exact proper performance from those conducting it ["The Valor of Ignorance," in Ernest W. Lefever, ed., *Morality and Foreign Policy: A Symposium on President Carter's Stance* (Washington: Ethics and Public Policy Center, 1977), p. 30].

35. For an excellent discussion of this point, see Jeane Kirkpatrick, "Dictatorships and Double Standards: A Critique of U.S. Policy," *Commentary,* November 1979; Reprint 22, Ethics and Public Policy Center, Washington, D.C.

# Index of Names

Abbot, Lyman, 13
Abernathy, Ralph, 42
Afghanistan, 33, 85, 86
Africa, 79, 86
Ahlstrom, Sydney, 4, 5
America, Latin, 29
Amish, 93
Anderson, John, 11
Angola, 85
Anti-Semitism, 15
Aquinas, Thomas, 16, 23, 24, 31
Arendt, Hannah, 27
Aristotle, 23, 24, 32, 33, 38, 62, 90
Armstrong, Samuel C., 97
Aron, Raymond, 89
Asia, 28, 79
Aspaturian, Vernon, 85
Associate Reformed Presbyterians, 104
Augustine, Saint, 22, 23, 29, 33
Auschwitz, 38
Austria, 81

Babel, 77
Baptists, 17, 42, 101, 103
*Barbarism the First Danger* (Horace
  Bushnell), 5
Barnes, Roslyn, 19
Bauer, P. T., 37
Becker, Carl, 25
Beckermann, Wilfred, 37
Belgium, 31, 59, 92
Bell, Daniel, 15
Belloc, Hilaire, 36, 56
Beria, Lavrenti Pavlovich, 84
Bismarck, Otto von, 27
Blair Bill, 102
Blake, William, 56
"Blake-Pike proposal," 2
Bochenski, J. M., 32
Boston, 97
Brezhnev Doctrine, 85, 86
Briefs, Goetz, 36, 37
"Buddhist Economics," 36
Bull, Hedley, 74, 75
Burke, Edmund, 37, 67
Bushnell, Horace, 5, 15

Caesar, 24, 39, 71
Calvin College, 4
Calvin, John, 72
Calvinism, 3, 17
Castle Island, 102
Catholic Society of St. Vincent de Paul,
  97
Charles I, King, 45
Chervonenko, S. V., 85
Chesterton, G. K., 23, 29, 36
Chicago, 95, 97
Chile, 85
China, 30, 37
*Christian America, A* (Robert Handy), 5
Christian Democratic parties, 31
Christian-Marxist movement, 33
*Christianity Today,* 3
Church of England (Anglican), 2, 101
*Church of the Holy Trinity* v. *U.S.*, 5
City of God, 22, 25
Civil War (U.S.), 88, 97, 102
Clergy and Laity Concerned, 42
Clinton, DeWitt, 101
Coffin, William Sloane, Jr., 42
Comenius, John Amos, 97
Constitution (U.S.), 31, 52, 76
Consultation on Church Union (COCU), 2
Conway, Monsignor, 19
Cotton, John, 45
Cuba, 29, 33
Czechoslovakia, 29, 85, 86

Declaration of Independence, 76
Democratic party, 11, 12
Dempsey, Bernard, S. J., 36
Deutsch, Karl, 80
Devlin, Lord, 41, 42, 49
Dickens, Charles, 56
*Divini Redemptoris* (Pius XI), 33
Dubcek, Alexander, 33
Dunkers, 93
Durkheim, Emile, 1
Dworkin, Ronald, 41, 49

Eliot, T. S., 56
Elliott, William Yandell, 65

---

*Note:* This index was prepared by Richard E. Sincere.

# Ethics and Public Policy Reprints

**Reprints are $1 each. Postpaid if payment accompanies order.**
**Orders of $10 or more, 10 per cent discount.**